Grandma Was Right!

39½ Slogans To Raise Children By

Anne McKay Garris

Grandma Was Right!
39 ½ Slogans To Raise Children By

Copyright 1997 by Anne McKay Garris
Published by *Studio 4 Productions*
Post Office Box 280400
Northridge, CA 91328-0400

Library of Congress Catalog Card Number: 96-69486

International Standard Serial Number 1-882349-60-1

Text Art: Dan Rosandich

Cover Art: Robert Howard

Book Design: *AV Communications*, Mesa, Arizona

Second Printing, revised, 1996

Printed in the United States of America

TABLE OF CONTENTS

Dedicated to

Nancy and Berle, Jr.
Who continue to bring us joy

And

Berle, Sr.
Whose love and common sense sustain us all

Foreword

by

H. S. Parker
Principal, Lejeune High School
Camp Lejeune, North Carolina

When you begin to read a book on raising children, the first question is, "How did the author's children turn out?" Having known both the Garris children since they were small, I believe I am qualified to answer that question.

In a practical sense, no one is more qualified to write about children and parenting than Anne Garris. She and Berle, Sr., her husband for more than forty years, have worked together to do an exemplary job of rearing their son and daughter. In addition, other children, including my own two sons, have had the privilege of having Anne and Berle as that vital set of second parents. Their influence has helped produce outstanding teenagers, a number of Eagle Scouts, and some excellent husbands and wives.

Even today, Anne continues to weave her magic with children. Her four grandchildren have enjoyed numerous sessions of "Granny Camp" on Clearwater beach. Under her tutelage they have learned about the wonders of nature, trekking up and down the coastline of Central Florida. It is interesting to hear the children nonchalantly identify the birds flying overhead, recite the names of the seashells lying in the sand, and make sensible comments about improving the ecological balance on the seashore.

Anne has done her most important teaching by precept and example. She emphasizes the importance of friendship by being a best friend to a number of people. She has taught her children and grandchildren about good citizenship by her constant involvement in current political issues, and along the way she has used her own life to help her children, grandchildren, and many of her friends come to a better understanding of the importance of trust, honesty, and integrity in our personal lives and in society. For that, many of us are truly thankful.

Acknowledgments

The Little Engine That Could
and
I Think I Can, I Think I can
are trademarks of Platt & Munk, Publishers
and are used by permission of the publisher.

Excerpts from
My Raisin Has A Wrinkle
recorded by Dulcimer Dan & The Blue Skies Band
Used by permission of composer Rick Morgan
and performer Dan Gilvary
85 Timberland; Louisburg, North Carolina 27549
Copyright 1990

Introduction

Raising kids is a joyful and exciting adventure. At least it was until the news media, television, doctors and dentists, and even the school system began to portray parents as inept and inadequate, unsure of themselves and afraid of their kids. No wonder parents spend more time worrying about their ability to do a good job than enjoying the process.

This makes me very angry! I want to stand on a mountain top and shout to young parents everywhere, "You can do it! It's not that hard! Enjoy!" Not having a mountain top handy, I wrote this book instead.

It's my way of sharing an easy way to teach basic values to children. I know it works! In our family we used slogans, taught us by our parents and grandparents, not to mention aunts and uncles (although I confess to moments of confusion when my grandmother, who loved nonsense verses, recited such jewels as, "I eat my peas with honey. I've done it all my life. It makes my peas taste funny, but it keeps them on my knife.")

Slogans are quickly understood, easy to remember, and often good for a shared chuckle. We find they grab our offspring's attention, catching them unawares before they can roll their eyes or manage a super patient sigh of protest.

Using slogans as a parenting tool is not difficult. For us, it was doing what comes naturally. "Himself" (alias Berle Garris, Sr., my husband and partner in raising kids, and other dangerous activities) comes from a family where the emphasis is on common sense. My family, I'm afraid, is more given to nonsense. (Grandmother, who was excellent at quoting slogans, enjoyed nonsense like Shakespeare or Alice in Wonderland. Still making the family rounds is the story about the young granddaughter who, when asked to quote a Bible verse at Sunday School, said, "I eat my peas with honey. I've done it all my life. It makes my peas taste funny, but it keeps them on my knife.")

Nothing the astonished Sunday School teacher said could shake the child's belief that it was a Bible verse. After all, it was a Grandmother "saying."

Nevertheless, both of us inherited an abundance of memories which began with "Grandma always said...."

Grandma Was Right! is a timesaving reference book for busy parents, with lighthearted ideas for benevolent interfering by grandparents, aunts, uncles, and all other people who love children. Anyone can use it. Who doesn't need a reminder that "Forgiveness Is The Best Revenge," or that "Life By The Yard Is Hard, But Life By The Inch Is A Cinch?"

If your darling daughter is having a pity-me party, or your charming son is howling for revenge, there's no time to visit the library. Turn instead to the Index of Challenges in the back of *Grandma Was Right!* and find an uncomplicated way to deal with their attitudes. Our experience is, if you start early — and persist — slogans are most effective.

Here then, for what they're worth, are the slogans and sayings we used in raising our children. May you enjoy them as much as we have!

At the end of the book, there are blank pages for your own slogans, because someday, when you least expect it, your children, too, will admit, *"Grandma Was Right!"*

Incidentally, as you read *Grandma Was Right!,* you will discover very quickly that I gave up being a modest mother when Nancy, our oldest, was two weeks old. We have never thought of our children as perfect, but we do think they're wonderful. Grandma always said, "The birthright of every child should be parents who think they're wonderful — and say so."

Anne McKay Garris

All the talent and brains in the world will not help a person who never learned to say,

"I THINK I CAN!"

Remember the story book about "The Little Engine That Could" pulling the heavy load of toys?

He puffed his way over the mountain, saying, *"I think I can, I think I can, I think I can!"*

Help your little ones say it as they —
    Climb the stairs,
    Tie their shoes,
    Start school.

Better yet, find the book and read it to them.

And they'll be able to —
    Finish school,
    Find a job,
    Make a marriage work,
    ...Not to mention RAISE KIDS!

Saint Paul said, *"I can do everything through Him who gives me strength."*

Philippians 4:13 NIV

"I Think I Can, I Think I Can"

On a balmy Spring afternoon, Himself and I sat in our quiet back yard, having one of those rare "where did we go right" sessions parents occasionally enjoy. Nancy, our oldest, was a sophomore in college, making excellent grades, majoring in fashion merchandising and looking forward to marrying her Benjamin, a charming young man she had dated since her Junior High years. Well adjusted, sure of her goals and self-possessed, Nancy is a pleasure to have around.

Berle, our youngest, had just successfully completed the difficult task of obtaining an appointment to the United States Naval Academy. Ebullient, quick-witted and ready for adventure, he makes us proud to be his parents.

"How do you suppose it happened, in this uncertain world, that we've managed to raise two kids who not only seem to know what they want, but have the motivation to go after it?" my husband asked.

Nancy overheard him. She came skipping down the porch steps. "Oh, you know. It was that silly little book you kept reading us about that dumb little train that said, 'I think I can, I think I can, I think I can'!" She laughed and hugged her father.

The Little Engine That Could was a favorite of both Nancy and Berle and we read it to them dozens of times. It's about a little engine that didn't feel very useful until, one day, the big engine wouldn't start and the little engine was called upon to pull a train full of toys over the mountain to the children in the village. It was a hard job, but, according to the book, he kept chugging along, saying, "I think I can, I think I can..." until the task was done. My favorite part was at the end, when the little engine puffed down the other side of the mountain saying, "I thought I could, I thought I could..."

I don't remember either of the children ever saying, "I think I can..." when handed a difficult task, but they certainly reflected it in the way they tackled some of the important challenges that came their way. Mind you, they also blew some, but I've forgotten what they were.

You can't convince me that the books children read don't make a difference. Putting in their hands books which promote positive and helpful attitudes will have its effect.

Songs, too, are important. We taught them "Would You Like To Swing On A Star" and "Accentuate The Positive" as well as dozens of Sunday School songs, including "Be Careful Little Hands What You Do" and "This Little Light Of Mine" (I'm gonna let it shine!). Of course, their Grandma also taught them, "I'm a little prairie flower, growing wilder by the hour," and other nonsense songs. You couldn't do much with Grandma.

All of it adds up.

When our grandchildren reached the toddler stage, I found *The Little Engine That Could* in my favorite book store and bought three copies—one for each family and one for "Grandma's House." There's a lot to be said for learning early to say, "I think I can..."

If you want your kids to SAY "NO" TO DRUGS. . .

and other things like rude behavior, weird clothes, stealing, lying and cheating,

Teach them:

"EVERYBODY'S DOING IT DOESN'T MAKE IT RIGHT!"

Start early! When they throw sand from the sand box, roll in a mud puddle, ask to pierce their ears, use bad language.

To make it work, you too, must believe "'Everybody's doing it doesn't make it right!", and act like you believe it.

As St. Paul said: *"Do not conform any longer to the pattern of this world, but be transformed by the renewing of your mind in Christ Jesus."*
Romans 12:2 NIV

"'Everybody's Doing It' Doesn't Make It Right"

Nancy danced into the kitchen, slamming the door behind her. "Mother, there's a carnival at the shopping center. Can we go? Can we?" She grabbed my skirt, tugging it for emphasis. "Tim says there's rides and cotton candy and a merry-go-round. Please can we go?"

"Sure, Honey!" I looked over the pile of wash to be done. "We'll go—later. Maybe this afternoon after lunch."

Her face fell. "Oh Mother! Tim says everybody's going this morning. We'll be last! Please!" Her brown eyes managed to dance and plead at the same time.

I have to admit a carnival is more fun with your friends, so I set the wash aside and rounded up her brother from the back yard. We made the three block walk to the shopping center in record time and found the carnival just as Tim had described it. Except, where was Tim—and all the other neighborhood children? None of them were there.

Not that it mattered. The kids headed for the merry-go-round and, being a bit of a kid myself, I quickly joined the fun. Soon I discovered the neighborhood kids had come. I didn't notice the disgruntled looks from the other mothers until Tim's mother sat down beside me.

I offered her a hunk of cotton candy. "Having fun?" I asked.

"Well, yes," she said, "but I would have preferred to come this afternoon."

"This afternoon? Nancy said Tim was coming this morning."

"No, Tim told me Nancy was coming and he wanted to…. Oh, goodness!"

Mary's mother, arriving in time to hear the conversation, began laughing. "And Mary said she had to come this morning because Tim and Nancy were. Do you think we've been had by a bunch of preschoolers?"

Nancy and Berle were so pleased with the carnival that I let it go for the time being. Nevertheless, I kept thinking about being "had" by a preschooler. The next time my four-year-old told me she had to do something because everyone else was doing it, I sat her down beside me.

"Nancy, my love," I said, "you're not too young to learn that 'everybody's doing it' is no reason for doing anything. If you have another reason, we'll talk about it."

Looking down the years, I could see my children saying, "But, Mother, everybody else was trying drugs—stealing hubcaps—cheating on their exams—getting married at fourteen."

It seemed to me there was no time like the present to prevent that kind of conversation. "'Everybody's Doing It' Doesn't Make It Right" became our family motto, for both adults and children. The only reason I didn't do it in needlepoint to hang over our mantel was because I don't do needlepoint.

Years later, when we were in a new community, Nancy was invited to a party by a young man we didn't know well. As she dressed for the evening, I was distinctly nervous and trying not to show it.

"Nancy, Honey," I said, "please remember tonight, 'Everybody's Doing....'"

"I know, Mother, I know!" Her voice was impatient but I knew she heard me. Long habit would protect her. No matter what her new friends were like, no matter what activities they suggested, I knew she would hold to her own standards. She never disappointed me!

We, too, tried not to disappoint her or her brother. One very hot sunday, Himself and I were discussing whether or not he should go to church in his shirt sleeves. Eventually he said, "I might as well, the others are all doing it!"

"'Everybody's doing It' Doesn't Make It Right," chorused the children. We all laughed. And Daddy kept his coat on.

I wondered if I had overdone it the day Nancy said, hesitantly, "Mother, I know '"Everybody's Doing It" Doesn't Make It Right,' but all the girls at school are wearing these pretty, frilly blouses."

"Oh my goodness!," I thought. "'Everybody's doing it' doesn't make it wrong, either."

On the way to the store to look for a frilly blouse, we made a game of deciding all the reasons for buying the blouse that had nothing to do with "everybody."

Although conformity, especially among teenagers, is normal and most of it harmless, it can lead to the horror of young people following the gang into doing all the dreadful things they manage to do to themselves in order to belong. I believe that nature pushes young people to a certain amount of conformity regardless. They need strong counter-pressure from people they respect in order to have the courage to make their own choices.

Unfortunately, peer pressure is such a strong, innate force, it's tempting to use it to promote desirable behavior. I know a mother who found herself discouraging her first-grader from wanting an expensive lunch box with, "Why don't you wait and see what the other kids are going to use? You wouldn't want to be the only one with a gorilla-shaped box, would you?"

"So what am I teaching him?" she asked me. "Copy your friends? Just last week I persuaded him to wear a dress-up shirt to a birthday party because all the other boys would be wearing one. I can't believe I did it."

It seems so innocent to urge conformity on young children, but being taught, when they're young, to do anything because someone else is doing it, can cause real trouble later, even into adulthood. Witness the politicians, caught misusing public money, who hide behind the excuse that all the other politicians are doing it.

I have never regretted insisting that our children think of better reasons for doing something than "Everybody's doing it." Far from being ostracized because of it, they developed the self-confidence to be leaders.

The habit of believing "'Everybody's Doing It' Doesn't Make It Right," taught early, can prevent a lot of heartache when they're older. It also helps if they can watch their parents set their own standards without regard to "everybody else."

The best advice for relationships is:

"TREAT OTHERS AS YOU WOULD LIKE TO BE TREATED"

Easy to Remember — Hard to Do!

YOU KNOW THE DRILL. . .

"Mother, Mary took my blouse; I'm going to kill her!"

"No you're not! You're going to treat her as you would like to be treated!"

"Dad, my teacher is a dull, prejudiced goonbug. I'm gonna put chewing gum in his shoe."

"No, son. You should treat him as you would like him to treat you."

"Grandma, Betty called me a big, bossy buffoon. What should I do?"

"Why not treat her as you'd like to be treated? Tell her she's a beautiful, blessed benefactress."

"What's a benefac. . . huh?"

"So in everything," Jesus commanded, *"do to others what you would have them do to you, for this sums up the Law and the Prophets."*
Matthew 7:12 NIV

"Treat Others As You Would Like To Be Treated"

The Golden Rule—"Do unto others as you would have them do unto you"—is the "slogan" which Jesus used to sum up all the rules of life and love. We shortened it to "Treat others as you would like to be treated." The children heard about it early—and often.

When Berle was in his teens, he and his best buddy had their one and only quarrel. It was over a girl both of them liked. That they would argue over anything came as a shock to Berle. These two were the best of buddies, accustomed to spending long hours out on the water, skiing together.

The morning after the quarrel dawned bright and clear. We looked out on mirror smooth waters, perfect for skiing. Any other morning and Berle's friend would have been on the doorstep, urging him to hurry up and get the skis in the boat.

"Mom, what should I do?" He was close to tears.

"Try the Golden Rule," I suggested. "If he had the boat and you had the skis, what would you want him to do?"

"I'd want him to ignore the whole thing," he said, on his way to the phone. "Pretend like it never happened!"

Minutes later the two friends were out on the water together and, so far as I know, the subject was never discussed between them again.

Sometimes it's interesting to stop and visualize what this world would be like if everyone, or just the majority of people, treated others the way they'd like to be treated. What a hotbed of understanding, patience and goodwill we would have!

All of us learn some version of the Golden Rule somewhere along the way. (At our house, some smart-aleck always added, "Do unto others, but do them first.") In the hurly burly of life, with so many emotions running rampant and so much ego to feed, it's hard to stop and think, "How would this person like to be treated?" Answering that question takes time and patience and practice—lots of it!

Like most of our "sayings," this one works both ways. Have you noticed how seldom adults treat children as they would like to be treated? Our hand on their shoulder, we say, "Johnny is shy about meeting new people." Or, "Patsy knows we don't want her to eat sweets because she's overweight." It's as though they are either deaf or have no feelings.

We nag them constantly. We correct them in public. In short, we treat them in a way that would be most offensive to any grown-up.

If we can treat our children as we would want to be treated, if we offer the Golden Rule as the best way to deal with their relationships, then we will give them a key to solving the most important challenge in their lives—how to get along well with others.

"I'm gonna get even with Jeff. . ."

"We're gonna make Betty pay for her meanness. . ."

"Lindsey's gonna be sorry. . ."

"Tommy is going to get it good. . ."

"Wait 'til I'm through with Harry. . ."

Revenge is sweet to contemplate, disastrous to carry out.

Try to teach children that

"FORGIVENESS IS THE BEST REVENGE"

They might not believe you, but if they try it, they will find forgiveness sets them free from Anger, Frustration, Retribution, Wasted Energy, Fear, Wasted Time, Loss of Friends and a possible stomach ulcer.

Jesus said, *"But if you do not forgive men their sins, your Father will not forgive your sins."*

Matthew 6:15 NIV

"Forgiveness Is The Best Revenge"

"She did it again, Mother! She's mean as a snake!" Slamming the door behind him, our son and heir came into the kitchen, his eyes flaming with anger, his face flushed with frustration

Himself spared only a raised eyebrow for the forbidden door slamming. "I take it we're speaking of Miss Snelling." His voice was deceptively mild.

Finding his father unexpectedly on the premises, Berle struggled for a show of dignity. Drawing himself up to his full four feet, ten inches, he lifted his chin.

"She punished the whole class because Ralph Logan threw an eraser," he said. "She does it all the time, but she won't do it any more. We're making plans," he added mysteriously.

"Like what?" asked my husband, managing to keep a straight face.

"A petition to the principal; glue in the lock of her cabinet and, er...."

"And...?"

"Well, maybe a snake in her desk drawer." His caution increasing under his father's steady gaze, he added, "Nothing poisonous, Dad. Just a little garter snake."

Glad Himself was around for this one, I hid a smile. I could picture the conference on the school bus. Joey, breathless with indignation, surely offered the snake. Larry's creative mind no doubt produced the idea of glue in the lock, and our future diplomat probably suggested the petition as the least damaging solution.

I knew the teacher wasn't basically unkind, just a poor disciplinarian. She had a tendency to let children get away with murder until chaos developed, then punish them all for some small infraction. They never knew when the axe would fall.

It was an unsettling year for Berle. He never minded obeying the rules. He only wanted to know what they were. Himself and I had talked about the problem, so I bit my tongue and waited.

"Sounds interesting," said his father. "Grab a soda and let's talk about it."

Wary at sweet reasonableness from this unexpected source, Berle took a drink from the refrigerator and slid into a seat at the kitchen table.

"I have a better idea than snakes, glue and petitions," said Himself. "Why not forgive Miss Snelling? Being a teacher is hard work."

"Forgive her! You've gotta be kidding!" Berle sloshed his soda. He grabbed a napkin, making furious jabs at the spill. "She's mean, Dad, someone has to stop her."

"Okay! Okay!" His father picked up a pad and pencil.

"Let's see. Glue, one tube, 75¢." He read out loud as he wrote. "Petition, printing, $2.00...."

"So what? I've got money."

"Money no problem," wrote Himself. "Other consequences— snake in desk drawer, probably two weeks' suspension."

"It's Joey's snake."

"Joey's snake." The pen moved swiftly. "One week's suspension for knowing about snake in desk and not reporting it."

"Dad!"

"And three weeks' loss of allowance."

"Dad!"

"Well, son, what kind of parents would we be not to respond to your suspension from school? Would you rather we grounded you for three weeks?"

"No!" The fight was gone out of him. "But, Dad, it's just not fair, the way she treats us."

Himself put his arm around the small shoulders. "Life frequently isn't fair, son," he said. "You can waste a lot of time and frustration on things that aren't fair. That's why you need to learn Forgiveness Is The Best Revenge. The best thing to do is turn it over to a higher power."

"You mean pray about it?"

"Well, yes, but this time you probably don't need to go that high. I'm sure your mother already has plans to deal with your teacher's unfairness."

Yeah, thanks, I thought, knowing he was right.

"Forgiving isn't easy," his dad continued, "but it beats wasting time on plots and plans, anger and frustration, not to mention getting yourself into trouble. Now," he added, "instead of wasting our time writing petitions, why not shoot a round of skeet? I came home early so we'd have time before dark."

Getting even is hard work and seldom worth the trouble. No wonder they call it "nursing" a grudge. We tried to help our children see that forgiving someone takes away that person's power over you, setting you free, mentally and emotionally, to pursue better things. Even for adults, the urge to get even is strong and "Forgiveness Is The Best Revenge" may seem a paradox—except to those who've tried it.

"Hey, Dad, I've got a problem," they say.

"IS IT A PROBLEM OR AN UNSOLVED OPPORTUNITY?", you say.

First thing you know, they'll be—
    Wowing professors and bosses,
    Impressing spouses,
    Solving problems,
    Taking care of themselves,
    Looking out for others,

And just possibly,
    Setting the world on fire!

There's a big difference between a person who deals with problems and one who deals with "opportunities."

"Some people find a challenge in every difficulty; others find a difficulty in every challenge."

Aunt Nellie

"Is It A Problem Or An Unsolved Opportunity?"

I have found that behavior can usually be controlled with discipline. "If you hit your sister again, you must go to your room," makes sense. Teaching attitudes is not so easy. "If you don't understand that your sister plays with your toys because she wants to be near you, I'm going to spank you," is hard to enforce. We found that slogans helped.

Himself has his own way of influencing attitudes. When the little ones came to their daddy, saying, "I've got a problem," the answer was, invariably, "Do you have a problem, or an unsolved opportunity?"

What a terrific attitude to teach a child! With their daddy's help, our two turned a lot of problems, large and small, into opportunities.

At the tender age of ten, young son felt he had the problem of more financial needs than his allowance could meet. His father, treating it as an unsolved opportunity, offered him the loan of the family lawn mower if he wanted to go out and seek his fortune in the lush grass of our neighbors. With his chin reaching barely above the mower handle, he trundled it down the street in search of jobs. He soon had a healthy clientele and even healthier pocketbook. He finished the summer with a sizeable bank account and the knowledge that a new baseball bat equals X number of hours of hard work.

Mind you, when the children were teenagers and trying their wings, this attitude presented us with our own "unsolved opportunities." Very often the "problem" was that we said no to something they wanted to do. Our offspring treated this as an unsolved opportunity, setting their minds to the task of persuading us to change ours. It made their teenage years interesting. It also established a habit of using creative ways to reach their goals.

Years later, struggling with the extraordinary challenge of making the grade at the United States Naval Academy, Berle had an appointment with one of his professors. He needed assistance in a class that was almost more than he could handle. To make matters worse, he and the professor were somewhat less than compatible. Berle dreaded the interview.

The professor kept him standing. "Well, Mr. Garris," he said, "do you have a problem?"

Without even thinking, our son responded, "I don't know if it's a problem or an unsolved opportunity."

The gruff professor stared in astonishment, then broke into a smile. "An unsolved opportunity," he said. "I like that! You'll do fine here with that kind of attitude."

And he did, too!

"Oh goodness, I need to go to the bathroom, but they won't stop talking, and I'm not supposed to interrupt. What can I do? Oh, dear!"

I know!

"PFFT PFFT PFFT PFFT"

"Son, what is that noise you're making?"

"I'm sorry, Mom. That's what a word sounds like going in edgewise."

"Well, tell me, what does pfft, pfft, pfft mean going in head on?"

"It's just that, well, I gotta go!"

"Oh! Why didn't you say so?"

Auntie says, *"If you don't listen to children, what makes you think they'll listen to you?"*

"Pfft, Pfft, Pfft, Pfft"

Although, unlike our grandparents, we never believed children should be seen and not heard, it's hard to enjoy a conversation when children are constantly interrupting. In a family where everyone tends to talk at once this posed a dilemma until the day Himself came home with a story.

It seems a little boy went with his mother to visit his aunt. His interest in the toy his aunt provided for him waned quickly as conversation between the two sisters proceeded without pause. The youngster began to twist and turn on his small stool.

"Stop wiggling." His mother frowned briefly at him, then turned back to her sister.

Next the boy tried making patterns on the rug with the toe of his shoe.

"What is he doing to my rug?" His aunt reached down and stilled the motion of the small leg.

He tried sitting very still and thinking, but that didn't take long. Finally he began to make soft noises. Suddenly, his eyes lit up. "Pfft, Pfft, Pfft, Pfft." The sound was just loud enough to be heard. It gained him a glance from his mother. He turned up the volume, "PFFT, PFFT, PFFT, PFFT."

"Joe, whatever are you doing?" Interrupted in the middle of a delightful tale of scandal, his mother was truly annoyed.

"I'm just saying 'Pfft, Pfft, Pfft, Pfft'," he answered.

"And what does 'Pfft, Pfft, Pfft, Pfft' mean?" asked the aunt.

"Not much," he said. "It's just a word going in edgewise."

I'd like to report the sisters took the hint and found some entertainment for the youngster, but the story stops there. At least it did when we heard it.

Being able to say "Pfft" seemed a useful tool in our garrulous family where conversations frequently run into each other without pause. We had taught our children not to interrupt adult conversations. It seemed only fair to give them a tool to use when they needed our attention, or had something to say. There were guidelines, of course. An unspoken rule forbade the use of "Pfft, Pfft, Pfft," more than once every ten minutes. We also made it clear they could join the conversation, but not dominate it as children have been known to do. To me, the only thing worse than a child-dominated conversation is a parent's constant cry of, "Don't interrupt!" every time the child wishes to speak.

Pfft is a quiet little sound that doesn't really intrude. It allows the adults a chance to finish their train of thought before pausing to give the child their full attention. I can't remember a time when Nancy and Berle overdid it. Unless you count the time Himself and I were having a "vigorous discussion." Nancy interrupted with a "Pfft, Pfft, Pfft," distracting us sufficiently to end the argument. If she had used words "going in head on" we would probably have told her to mind her own business, or sent her from the room.

As they reached the age where it's legitimate for children to participate in adult conversations, ours used it to let us know they had something to add. This helped us find the right moment to say, "Nancy, did you want to comment on this?" Or, "Berle, do you want to tell Mrs. Jones your side of this story?" Frequently, the "Pfft" was so unobtrusive the other adults were not aware of it.

We feel it helped our children to be comfortable with talking to adults. At any rate, it is a fun way of solving a small problem. When the children were older, it was not uncommon for a chorus of "Pfft, Pfft, Pfft" to urge a termination point on a family member who was wearing out a subject.

Looking back, I'm grateful my parents encouraged my siblings and me to be a part of adult conversations instead of dismissing us from the room. I've learned a lot since the time my mother gently chided me for reading a book while a guest related his experiences in the mission field.

"You missed some wonderful stories about what people are like in Korea," she said. "Next time, put down your book and listen."

In our family we expect general conversations to be free of language and topics unsuitable for children. This makes it possible to encourage the children to take part. It's a valuable learning process in the area of good communication.

Recently, the extended family gathered for a meal. We remained at the table long after dinner was over, involved in a lively visit, covering a broad range of topics. When time came to leave, Nathan, our twelve-year-old grandson, looked around him in surprise.

"I liked that!" he said. "I've always jumped up from the table as soon as I finished eating, but I actually enjoyed this. I didn't know grown-ups could be so interesting."

He had been very much involved in the conversation. Knowing at a very young age how to use Pfft, Pfft, Pfft, to "get in a word edge-wise" probably helped.

"Why can't I hit him?"

"Why can't I climb the tower?"

"Why can't I play in the street?"

Children are entitled to REASONS but one too many "whys" deserves the answer,

"BECAUSE I SAY SO!"

It may be Old Fashioned, but it reassures the little ones that Somebody Big is in charge.

St. Paul Writes, *"Children obey your parents in the Lord, for this is right."*

Ephesians 6:1 NIV

"Because I Say So"

When Berle was a lively two-year-old, we visited friends in Georgia. He had more than the usual enthusiasm and curiosity for which that age is noted and containing my young bundle of energy in someone else's home was a challenge. My conversations with him were liberally sprinkled with "No" and "Don't" and "Stop."

Our hostess gently remonstrated with me. "We want our little one to be raised hearing only positives," she said. "We try never to use 'Don't' or 'No' or 'Stop' in talking to her."

She was right! I watched in awe as she quietly guided her tiny daughter away from mischief and danger.

"Mother wants you to play with these spoons," she said, "instead of that sharp old knife." Or, "Please come and punch the teddy bear, dear, instead of Berle. He didn't mean to hug you too tight."

Her efforts to use only positive words were impressive. Her daughter was charming and unspoiled.

Then came the twins! The next time we visited, the twins were toddling after their big sister and the sounds of "No" and "Don't" fell often from their mother's lips as her brood scattered in all directions, usually with mischief in mind.

It's nice to try to be always positive in dealing with our children, but sooner or later all parents have to play the heavy.

In this case, it was just as well the mother learned to say, "No!" Once they've learned the meaning of no, it's time to go on to bigger and better things, like asking, "Why?" Conscientious parents can get beaten at this game in a hurry.

"No, Honey, we can't play with knives. Give it to Mother."

"Why?"

"Because it's sharp and might hurt you, or someone else."

"Why?"

"Well, because..."

It can go on forever if you don't call a halt and the best halt I know is, "Because I Say So."

The last time Berle played, "Why?" with me, he was senior patrol leader of his Scout Troop. I repeated to him his dad's instructions that he could not go on a planned camp-out because the weather was getting nasty. Berle dragged out all the arguments he could invent and I batted them down, one at a time, then put him on the phone to his father. They went through the same question and answer routine and Berle finally admitted defeat.

With his scout master out of town and not due back until time to move out, the final decision on going was up to Berle as senior patrol leader. Reluctantly, he began calling the Scouts to let them know the plans were canceled. He found himself on the other side of the conversation while Scouts argued with him. After a frustrating forty minutes he put down the phone.

"Mother," he said, "is this how you feel when I argue with you?"

"Probably," I answered.

"I've been their senior patrol leader for a year. They elected me. Why can't they just trust my judgment instead of asking all those questions?"

"Why indeed?" I said. "Have you tried, Because I Say So?"

Laughing, he crossed the room, gave me a hug and went back to the telephone, patiently answering all the arguments and questions his fellow Scouts threw at him. After that, I don't recall any extensive arguments with our son that began with "Why."

As charter vice-president of The Society For The Prevention Of Cruelty To Mothers, I steadfastly insist on a parent's right to use "Because I said so!" To be deprived of using this last resort argument stopper is cruel and unusual punishment for anyone in charge of a child.

Of course we need to give our children reasons for our decisions on their behalf. Of course we need to let them test their talents for persuasion on us. But we are also entitled to defend ourselves against the creeping insanity of conversations that degenerate into "Why" on their part and endless explanations on ours.

"Because I Said So!" is every parent's constitutional right. Use it with confidence!

"DON'T SWEAT THE SMALL STUFF"

is good for gaining perspective on the GIANT TRAGEDIES in their lives —

- like breaking a fingernail,
- getting the ball stuck on the roof,
- not finding their favorite jeans.

BUT USE THIS WITH CARE! They might tell you "Don't Sweat The Small Stuff" when you yell about —

- neglected home work,
- late hours,
- small dents in the car's fender.

Jesus reassures us, *"Look at the birds of the air; they do not sow or reap or store away in barns, and yet your heavenly Father feeds them. Are you not of more value than they?"*

Matthew 6:26 NIV

"Don't Sweat The Small Stuff"

I don't know where they got it, but "Don't Sweat The Small Stuff" came home from school with the kids. I'm sure it was Berle who started it. Nancy would never have adopted so inelegant a phrase.

As a mother who daily read articles about the well brought-up youngsters who suddenly turned to drugs, skipping school, and all sorts of evils including not bathing, I did tend to get uptight over the smallest sign of noncompliance with family standards.

I was in the midst of a top scream tirade one day over some small infraction of the rules when my son interrupted with, "Hey, Mom, Don't Sweat The Small Stuff!"

Into my stunned silence he charged. "Mother, dear," he said, "I'm sorry! I shouldn't have worn those ragged jeans to school. I didn't know it would upset you so. I won't do it again. But please save your high decibels for the biggies and Don't Sweat The Small Stuff. You'll be old before your time."

A fast hug and kiss saved him from the swat he deserved. The damage was done, though. He had handed me an excellent tool to deal with this child, so like his mother, who was easily upset over small things. I found "Don't Sweat The Small Stuff" a wise admonition in regard to petty injustices heaped on his head by uncaring authority, small setbacks in his search for academic excellence, and annoyances bestowed on him by everyone from his sister to passing strangers.

"Don't Sweat The Small Stuff" became one of our most used slogans during the exciting teen years, except that this one was never used on Himself. If he felt something was important enough to yell about, none of us dared call it small.

All of us have known people who get all "het up" about small things that will, or should be, forgotten almost immediately. They are among the most tiresome people I know. I avoid them if I can. How much better to learn early to serenely ignore the small irritations and frustrations of life—the "small stuff"—thus saving energy to get upset about the things that really matter, the things we can, and should, do something about.

When things go wrong and we're feeling sad, all of us need to be able to say,

"I NEED SOME TLC"

Tender Loving Care can make life easier when —

- we've been naughty,
- a friend has moved away,
- a pet has died,
- or life is just plain miserable.

Somehow, using the intials makes it easier to say, "I need some loving!"

"How long, O Lord? Will you forget me for-ever? ...But I trust in your unfailing love; my heart rejoices in your salvation."
Psalm 13:1, 5 NIV

"I Need Some TLC"

Nancy was a big grown girl the last time she plopped down in her daddy's lap and said, "I need some TLC." His response was immediate. With a kiss and a hug, he snuggled her into his arms and said, "Want to talk about it?"

"No," she said. "I'm not sure what's the matter. I just feel out of sorts and in need of some loving." The fact that leaving home for college was imminent may have prompted her malaise, but her independent soul refused to acknowledge it. It didn't matter. For years we had made sure that Tender Loving Care was in large supply in our family with no questions asked. Her father poured an avalanche of encouragement on her, telling her how loved and appreciated she was, how much we were going to miss her. He proposed a few tentative plans for her first visit home. Shortly, she went on her way, comforted.

We discovered TLC when Nancy was just a little girl. Great Aunt Sallie Lu brought some home from the hospital in a bottle. Her "TLC" was the most aromatic body lotion I've ever used. It was great for giving soothing back rubs that produced a mood of high contentment. The kids liked the lotion so it didn't last long, but the family latched on to the letters for Tender Loving Care and made them our own.

"I Need Some TLC" became a way to say difficult things like, "I'm not very happy with myself right now and need someone to love me," or "I can't love me. Please, you do it," or "It's hard to bear the hurt I gave you, Please take me back."

I cherish memories of the small, tear-stained faces of just-chastised little ones, asking boldly for a return to grace with, "Mommy, I need some TLC." Naturally, they always got a hug, and life was quickly good again for both of us.

When someone was being difficult, we tried to remember to ask, "Do you need some TLC?" It says, "I know your lousy actions are caused by something that's hurting you. I care enough to look behind your behavior and try to help—or just love you if I can't help."

Of course, there's always the chance that the response will be, "I don't need any of your old TLC. Just leave me alone!" We heard it more than once. No matter. They still got the message they were loved.

We tried to teach the children that people need love the most when they're most unlovable. When you're feeling unloved and un-lovely, or just out of sorts with the world, it's difficult to find the right words to tell someone about it. Too often, pride and hurt get in the way. We wanted them to be able to communicate their need for love.

I've often thought how much estrangement, loneliness, unforgiveness, mental illness, crime and just plain meanness could be avoided if all of us knew how to admit, "I need some TLC."

Pick, pick, pick — Why can't they get along?

Suggest they **"Put a little love in it"**

Complain, complain, complain — Their friends are not perfect.

Recommend they **"Put a little love in it"**

Whine, whine, whine — No chore is done without it.

Insist they **"Put a little love in it"**

You're at the end of your rope — the kids are driving you crazy. Remember the bottom line for raising children and

"PUT A LITTLE LOVE IN IT"

Saint Paul reminds us, *"Love is patient, love is kind. It does not envy, it does not boast, it is not proud. It is not rude, it is not self-seeking, it is not easily angered, it keeps no record of wrongs."*

1 Corinthians 13:4 NIV

"Put A Little Love In It"

My friend Mary's kitchen was large and, on this particular evening, full of kids—five of hers and two of mine, scurrying about like seven large ants. In the midst of this melee, Mary was preparing a dinner in honor of her son's birthday, with what help I could supply. Our husbands lounged in the living room, discussing weighty matters, oblivious to the steady stream of children past their feet.

"How in the world do you do it?" I asked Mary, marveling at her ability to work quietly in spite of the hullabaloo. Before she could answer, Tom, the birthday boy, was brought up short by the beautiful birthday cake on the counter, carefully decorated by Mary the day before. Tempted by the mounds of sugary icing, his fingers had already hooked a sweet morsel when his mother spotted him.

"Tom, stop that!" Her voice was sharper than she intended, startling him. Even as he savored the sweet on his tongue, a big tear rolled down his cheek.

"Mary," her husband, Dick, called from his place on the sofa, "Put A Little Love In It."

Mary's indignant look, aimed at the living room, was so brief I'm not sure it happened.

She smiled, and hugged her son. "It's your birthday, love. Do you want your cake now?" she asked.

When he nodded, she placed the cake on the kitchen table, handing each of the seven children a fork. "Happy birthday," she said. "Go for it."

While we continued dinner preparations, the children happily trashed the cake and spoiled their appetites. As the men came to dinner, Dick surveyed the scene with approval. "Now that's a birthday party!" he said. "One they'll always remember."

Although we never got around to a cake free-for-all at our house, we did make good use of "Put A Little Love In It." It was used to help remind the children why they were washing the dishes or picking up their toys, and who they were arguing with when they got into sibling rivalry exercises. It didn't stop many quarrels, but it helped us all to pull our punches.

Like Dick and Mary, we also used it to remind each other that raising kids is about love—not perfect birthday cakes, or spotless houses, or outstanding grades.

Mary and Dick raised a close knit, loving family. "Put A Little Love In It" surely helped.

Working together leads to communication. Communication leads to understanding. Understanding leads to sharing. Sharing leads to a feeling of belonging. And a feeling of belonging leads to knowing you are loved. Knowing you are loved—

- prevents a multitude of problems,
- solves a multitude of problems,
- makes life worth living.

Find a task — Invent one if you have to — Gather the family together, hand them a brush or a dish sponge or screwdriver. Tell them,

"MANY HANDS MAKE LIGHT WORK"

Use bribery, threats, coercion if necessary. You'll cement relationships and create memories.

"*Carry each other's burdens,*" says St. Paul, "*and in this way you will fulfill the law of Christ.*"

Galatians 6:2 NIV

"Many Hands Make Light Work"

My grandmother was an ardent believer in the philosophy of "Do it ourselves." She had more ideas and ambitions than one small, energetic person could possibly carry out alone, so her battle cry was, "Many Hands Make Light Work!"

Cooking a meal, making cookies, picking blackberries or pulling weeds, she invariably gathered all available grandchildren around her to help with the task. At the first sign of flagging enthusiasm she would sing out, "Many Hands Make Light Work," relentlessly maneuvering the would-be goof-offs back to the job.

Looking back, I cherish the times we spent together "making light work." I value the extra skills I learned, working as a team with Grandmother and my cousins—or whoever we could drag into it. As our children grew up, it seemed natural to adopt the philosophy that a shared task is not only easier, but more fun.

In our little family we found "Many Hands Make Light Work" should be used both ways. We tried to balance a request for help with the dishes, or raking the lawn, with an offer of assistance with bike repair or a picnic lunch for a teenage outing.

I confess it was a challenge to get everyone working on a shared task. Our success often depended on how much bribery was involved.

Knowing a swim in the lake must wait until camp was completely set up, we became an efficient team, raising the tent and arranging the gear in record time. Leaving the television off until supper dishes were done had many hands making light work of that task.

Part of the secret is to let them help when they volunteer, no matter how young or inept, even if this results in many hands actually making more work.

I must admit there were times when I no more convinced my children that "Many Hands Make Light Work" than Grandmother convinced some of us. The vegetable garden I attempted is a case in point. Although they enjoyed the results of my garden and helped when threatened or coerced, none of my family ever became a co-farmer. More's the pity. They don't know what they missed.

The culmination of Grandmother's belief that "Many Hands Make Light Work" eventually took root in all her grandchildren and passed on to her great-grandchildren. Long after she was no longer around to inspire us, her great-grandchildren, all nine of them young adults, gathered for Christmas vacation. They decided their Christmas present to their grandmother would be to redecorate her small Sea Shell Shop. With Nancy as taskmaster, they spent an entire day painting, repapering, rearranging and redesigning the shop as their grandmother bragged on them to the customers who braved the resulting chaos to come in.

There was much chatter and laughter among the cousins. Anyone who shirked was immediately dragged back to work with, "Come on now, 'Many Hands Make Light Work.' You don't want this to get too heavy, do you?"

They still chuckle over the incidents of that special day. Their grandmother still brags about it. For one, or two, it would have been a real chore. But "Many Hands Make Light Work," and often turn a hard task into a fond memory.

"Gee, Mom!" they say. Do I have to wash al-l-l those dishes?"

— or —

"You want me to baby-sit THREE WHOLE HOURS?!"

— or —

"I'll never pass that exam!"

— or —

"I'll never be old enough to . . . (whatever)"

They need to know —

"LIFE BY THE YARD IS HARD — LIFE BY THE INCH IS A CINCH"

Jesus said it this way: *"Therefore do not worry about tomorrow, for tomorrow will worry about itself. Each day has enough trouble of its own."*

Matthew 6:34 NIV

"Life By The Yard Is Hard,
Life By The Inch Is A Cinch"

"I'll never learn this piece." Berle slammed his fist on the piano in frustration, creating a sound wave that made me jump.

"Do that again, and you won't live long enough to learn it," growled his father.

"I've played it a jillion times and it just won't stick in my head," groaned our young pianist, already regretting his agreement to play for a class program.

"Practice a little bit at a time," I suggested. "Maybe that will help it stick."

"It's so boring," he said. "I'll never learn it all."

"Sure you will." My sympathy came from memories of my own efforts to memorize piano music. "Just remember—Life By The Inch Is A Cinch."

"And Life By The Yard Is Hard," he quoted, his hands moving again on the piano keys. Anything was better than listening to Mother lecture!

This slogan was posted on the bulletin board at Wesleyan Conservatory during exam week my senior year. Shakespeare, taught by one of the best teachers in the school, was everyone's dread. If Shakespeare said it, we had to memorize it. So I paid close attention.

The note on the bulletin board read:
Shakespeare on Exams:
"*Life By The Yard Is Hard.*
Life By The Inch Is A Cinch."

This thought got me through dozens of exam weeks, three broken hearts, many boring lectures, and one back injury. Later, it helped me through times of loneliness and worry, when Himself was in combat in Vietnam.

During one of these times, I realized how often, during the day, I had yelled at Nancy for no reason. She was only nine, for pity's sake, and I was expecting her to be a grown-up. At bedtime, I tried to apologize. "I'm sorry I was so cross with you today, Honey. I didn't mean to be!"

"It's all right, Mother." She reached up and patted my cheek. "You'll get a letter from Daddy tomorrow, and everything will be all right."

Life by the yard is hard. Taken one day at a time, it's easier. Sometimes, with God's help, you need to take it "moment by moment."

"Judy likes me one day and hates me the next."

"Bob says I'm off the team if I waste my time studying."

"If I win the prize, Barbara will be mad at me."

"Tim wants me to help him on his exams."

Make it plain —

"YOU DON'T NEED FRIENDS LIKE THAT"

Children need help choosing friends wisely...and they need help ending harmful friendships!

So do adults!

TOO MANY ADULTS HANG ON TO DE-STRUCTIVE FRIENDSHIPS.

TOO MANY CHILDREN FOLLOW THEIR EXAMPLE.

We need to change that. Just tell them, "You don't need friends like that!"

According to Proverbs, *"He who walks with the wise grows wise, but a companion of fools suffers harm."*

Proverbs 13:20 NIV

"You Don't Need Friends Like That"

Judy was a pretty little girl with big blue eyes and a charming personality. We were delighted when she made our Nancy welcome on her first day in a new school. Judy's lovely manners and good sense of humor made her visits to our home pleasant, and Nancy loved her as only an eight-year-old can love a friend. It was a while before we noticed something was wrong.

"Honey," I asked, "don't you like Judy anymore?"

"Well, yes," she said, "but Judy doesn't want me to be friends with anyone else. If I even speak to another girl Judy tells lies about me."

"Like what?" I asked.

"She told Mary I stole some money from her purse. Now Mary won't play with me. She told Linda I said something hateful about her. Mother, all the girls hate me." She burst into tears.

"What a little beastie!" I couldn't help myself.

"But now she's the only friend I've got."

"You Don't Need Friends Like That." I made it up on the spot, but it became one of our most needed sayings.

When Berle's friends called him "big brain" and "egg head," teasing him about his study habits, he became self-conscious about working hard at school.

"Maybe they're envious," I suggested. "Maybe they wish they could do as well."

"They don't want to," he said. "They brag about not studying."

"Is it important to you to make good grades?"

"Yeah, I guess so. I like to study. I even like to take exams." He seemed ashamed of it. "But that doesn't make me a sissy."

"I should say not! They're a bunch of jerks." I said it, and I'm glad. "Are you going to change habits, or friends?" I asked. "You Don't Need Friends Like That if they can't accept you as you are."

Berle didn't give up his friends right away, but he paid less attention to their teasing, gradually spending more time with classmates who were not threatened by his scholarship.

Rather than insist our children terminate a destructive friendship, we tried to give them a rationale for ending it on their own with, "You Don't Need Friends Like That."

"I don't want to be a snob," said a grown-up Nancy, "but I'm glad you taught me, 'You Don't Need Friends Like That.' It kept me from adapting my life-style or lowering my standards to keep a friendship. It's not worth it."

A true friend is a rare and valuable treasure, but people who use you for their own purposes are less than friends. One widely quoted definition of friendship is, "A friend is someone who accepts you as you are, but invites you to grow."

It's important to teach children to be kind and gracious to everyone, but the nature of a close friendship demands kindred spirits. No one needs a friend who consistently urges you to be less than you can be. Children who are taught, early, to seek friends who accept them as they are, will be less likely to give up everything worthwhile just to hold on to a friendship.

Still, it's tempting to continue a harmful friendship. Old friends are handy and new friendships are hard to establish. We read letters in advice columns from grown-ups who want to know how they can hold to their own code of conduct without losing a friend who doesn't share it.

The answer is obvious—you can't! Better to realize, "You Don't Need Friends Like That."

There's pain and distress in —
- An embarrassing moment,
- A stupid remark,
- An argument with a friend,
- A missed opportunity.

You think you'll feel it forever.

This leads to wrong decisions, lost happiness, time wasted in regret and, in severe cases, suicide or drug abuse.

Teach children early to PUT IT IN PERSPECTIVE.

Remind them —

"A HUNDRED YEARS FROM NOW, YOU'LL NEVER KNOW THE DIFFERENCE"

Or, as St. Paul said, *"Forgetting what is behind and straining towards what is ahead, I press on toward the goal to win the prize for which God has called me heavenward in Jesus Christ."*

Philippians 3:13-14 NIV

"A Hundred Years From Now You'll Never Know The Difference"

One of the hazards of youth is the unalterable conviction that today's tragedy or embarrassment, is a permanent condition with no hope of cure—ever. This ranges from incredible anguish over a mild case of acne to extremes of suicide and murder because of a failed exam or lost love. Like most teenage ailments, this is best prevented.

Aunt Sallie Lu, from the wisdom of her eighty years, offered the preventive medicine for this one.

"A Hundred Years From Now, You'll Never Know The Difference" was her comment on anything which threatened to upset the tenor of our days.

Nancy wore a dressy dress to a party where everyone else wore shorts. Showing off, Berle flipped the pizza off the table into the lap of a guest. Both events seemed like terrible calamities until they remembered, A Hundred Years From Now, You'll Never Know The Difference.

We even used it for romances and exams. "A Hundred Years From Now, You'll Never Know The Difference" may seem a heartless response to the end of a youthful romance. However, I'm thankful my parents refused to take my "broken hearts" seriously in my teenage years. (Actually, my parents were even more heartless. "Men Are Like Street Cars," they told me. "If you miss one there's always another one coming along.") It's hard to see your future as hopelessly blighted with the family taking bets on how soon you'll be madly in love again.

As for exams: Berle was distressed when I told him his sister was getting married the weekend between his exams at the Naval Academy.

"Oh, Mother, I can't come," he said. "If I miss exams, I'll flunk for sure!"

I didn't hesitate. "A Hundred Years From Now, You'll Never Know if you flunked an exam," I said firmly. "You will always regret missing your sister's wedding."

It took some doing, but he made it to the wedding. No one remembers how he did on the exams.

A young person who learns in grammar school how to deal with fluffed lines in the school play, embarrassing moments in class, and other momentary setbacks, will be more likely to survive the traumas of high school.

We were all aware of the obvious exaggeration in this slogan. Berle, who always planned to "be somebody" some day, was in agony over a stupid remark he made.

"Oh come on, Honey," I said. "A Hundred Years From Now, You'll Never Know The Difference."

"I don't know, Mom." He shook his head ruefully. "With my luck, it will be the lead story in my biography."

"Do you see that girl there? It's just awful! Do you know she (whisper, whisper, whisper)."

"Don't play with him. He's bad! He (whisper, whisper, whisper)."

"Mother, do you know, Mary is a mean tease?"

Where do they learn it? Maybe they hear —
- "Have you heard about the boss and his secretary?"
- "They are very good neighbors, but they (whisper, whisper, whisper)."

Now wait a minute! Don't you know,

"THERE'S SO MUCH GOOD IN THE WORST OF US, AND SO MUCH BAD IN THE BEST OF US, IT HARDLY BEHOOVES ANY OF US TO TALK ABOUT THE REST OF US"

As Jesus asked: *"Why do you look at the speck of sawdust in your brother's eye and pay no attention to the plank in your own eye?"*
Matthew 7:3 NIV

"There's So Much Good In The Worst of Us, And So Much Bad In The Best of Us, It Hardly Behooves Any of Us To Talk About The Rest of Us."

It is always pleasant to be around someone who is confident and secure enough to consistently speak well of others. It's also very rare! Gossip is contagious and insidious, with many disguises, making it easy to kid ourselves that we are "sharing information about our neighbors"—"just telling a good story"—"helping people understand their motives." Often the end result is the same as gossip. Someone gets hurt.

Children learn early to gossip for it comes naturally to all of us.

"Mother," said Nancy, "Betsy is a spoiled brat!"

"Who says so?" I was startled to hear my sweet young daughter repeating unkind words about her very pleasant friend.

"I heard Mrs. Watkins tell Mrs. Johnson," she replied.

"What do you mean by 'spoiled brat,'" I asked.

"I don't know." She moved uncomfortably away from me.

Taking her hands, I pulled her towards me. "Honey, if you don't know what it means, don't say it. If you find out it means something unkind, you still might not want to repeat it." I smiled into her big brown eyes. "Grandma always said, 'There's so much good in the worst of us, and so much bad in the best of us, it hardly behooves any of us, to talk about the rest of us.'"

She was intrigued. "Say that again," she demanded.

Slowly we repeated it together.

"What does it mean?" she wanted to know.

"Think about it," I told her, knowing we would be using the jingle often.

Gossip is so bad! It destroys friendships, businesses, reputations and marriages. It can undermine years of careful effort. It leaves the victims undefended and helpless. Yet it is seldom seen as the evil it really is.

If children's tales on their friends—or more likely their siblings—are greeted with, "Wait a minute. You need to remember, 'There's So Much Good In The Worst Of Us And So Much Bad In The Best Of Us, It Hardly Behooves Any Of Us To Talk About The Rest of Us,'" they are less likely to gossip and more likely to learn the pleasant habit of speaking well of others.

She's gorgeous — but you don't want her to depend on her looks.

He's handsome — but you want him to be much more.

Even you have to admit she's not pretty.

How can he get through those dreadful acne years?

It doesn't matter! When they want to know, "How do I look?", ask them,

"ARE YOU SMILING?"

A smile will light up a homely face,
Cover a multitude of blemishes,
Improve a beautiful face,
Make them pleasant to look at.

We read in Proverbs, *"A cheerful look brings joy to the heart..."*
Proverbs 15:30 NIV

"Are You Smiling?"

"Look, Mother, am I beautiful?" Nancy twirled around in her new Easter frock, her brown hair bouncing on her shoulders. Of course she's beautiful—I'm her mother! How do you answer a question like that?

I hesitated. At nine years old, my Nancy was already developing into a most attractive young lady and I wanted her to be self-confident in her looks without being vain.

Sensing my delay in answering, she stopped twirling. "Am I?" she asked, her eyes anxious.

"To me you are always beautiful." I pulled her into a bear hug. "Especially when a smile lights up those big brown eyes."

We've all seen women—and men—who depend on their beauty as a passport to acceptance and approval. How pitiful when that beauty fades and they feel they have nothing left. Still, children need all the help they can get to bolster their self-confidence. In a competitive world, knowing you are easy to look at helps. We tried to teach our children that wearing a smile is attractive, regardless of the arrangement of their features.

Nancy worried about a blemish on her face. "Try smiling and nobody will notice," we assured her.

Berle's hair was cut too short for his liking. "You'll just have to wear a big smile until it grows out," we told him. (This was asking a lot. Those were the days when short hair was very unstylish and woe be to the young man whose barber—or father—got carried away with the scissors.)

Even when Berle fell and chipped a piece off a front tooth, we assured him it would be less noticeable if he smiled. He bought it. Friends of mine were invariably surprised when I mentioned his chipped tooth. "I've never noticed," they'd say. "He has such a nice smile."

We tried to be truthful and generous with our compliments. Every girl needs to know her best features. Every boy needs to know he is good to look at in some way. We also tried to remember to add, "Especially if you smile," reminding them a genuine smile adds a pleasant touch to the nicest eyes and the most becoming outfit. It also helps with making friends. They discovered that for themselves.

Years later I found Nancy in front of the mirror, making faces at herself. Slipping up behind her, I made a few faces of my own.

"It really works, Mother." She sounded surprised.

"What works?" I asked.

"Frown into the mirror," she commanded. "Now smile. See, it does make you prettier."

"How 'bout that!" I faked amazement.

We laughed together in one of those moments a mother never forgets.

"EVERYTHING LOOKS BETTER AFTER A GOOD NIGHT'S SLEEP"

You know it...I know it...Everybody knows it.

So why do we let our children give us — and themselves — hassles at bedtime?

As of two hours before bedtime, every —
- Complaint
- Distress
- Problem
- Argument

— should be handled with the simple words, "Everything looks better after a good night's sleep."

After a good night's sleep, the Psalmist says, *"Let the morning bring me word of your unfailing love, for I have put my trust in you."*
Psalm 143:8 NIV

"Everything Looks Better After A Good Night's Sleep"

Nancy was close to tears. "Janie's mad at me. I'm never going to find time to hem my dress, and this geography is so stupid. I know I'll flunk the test tomorrow." She slammed her book down on the bed.

"Oh, come now," I soothed. "It can't be as bad as all that."

"It is, it is." She moaned. "Tomorrow will be a disaster."

There's only one cure for disaster. I gave her a warm hug and kissed her.

"Go to bed," I said. "Say your prayers. 'Everything Looks Better After A Good Night's Sleep.' We'll solve your problems in the morning."

The morning came early. I was wakened by a soft voice in my ear. "Mom! Wake up, Mom. If you'll drill me on my geography, I can hem my dress and study too."

We had a pleasant hour together. As we headed to the kitchen for breakfast, I asked her, "What about Janie?"

"What about Janie?" she asked.

"She's mad at you, remember."

"Oh, that! Pooh! She'll get over it. I'll just say I'm sorry."

For years we wasted hours trying to persuade our two that their problems were exaggerated by weariness at bedtime. I offered them solutions they refused to accept and drilled them for tests when they were too tired to learn.

Once we happened upon "Everything Looks Better After A Good Night's Sleep," we learned to offer love, sympathy and reassurance at night, saving advice and suggestions for the morning hours. Sometimes we threw in a back rub for good measure.

All problems, of course, aren't solved by a night's sleep, but even the toughest are easier to tackle with a refreshed mind in a rested body. I've discovered this is especially true if I've prayed about it, seeking God's will. Sometimes exciting solutions seem to simply be there waiting for me in the morning.

Now the children are grown, I'm not allowed to worry about anything at night, either. "Mother," they say, "go to bed now and call me in the morning. You know my mother always told me, 'Everything Looks Better After A Good Night's Sleep.' I love you, bye!"

After 30, it isn't partying that makes the world go 'round. It's volunteering —

- Church
- Hospice
- Little League
- Scouts
- Food Pantry
- Meals-on wheels
- Teacher's Aide
- Political Action
  — You name it......

When they ask you, "Why do you do it?", tell them what my Uncle Walton once said:

"SERVICE IS THE RENT YOU PAY FOR THE SPACE YOU OCCUPY"

Children who are not taught to serve others seldom get around to it as adults — and wonder why they're bored.

Jesus told his disciples: *"The greatest among you will be your servant."*

Matthew 23:11 NIV

"Service Is The Rent You Pay For The Space You Occupy"

A story I read long ago tells of a youngster whose father found him watching T.V. on a beautiful summer afternoon.

"Son," said the father, "would you rather watch a T.V. show you won't remember to the end of the week, or would you like to do something you'll remember all of your life?"

Thus enticed, the young man soon found himself out mowing the lawn of an elderly neighbor. His father was right. Years later, he still remembered the satisfaction of that bit of service, and the fervent appreciation of his neighbor.

Spread throughout the United States are hundreds of men who spent their Scouting days in my Uncle Walton Peabody's Boy Scout Troop. An enthusiastic Scout himself, Uncle Walton, with Aunt Louise's help, raised five boys. His enjoyment of Scouting was such that his Scout leadership both predated and postdated his sons' participation. He was a loving, enthusiastic Scout leader who believed that Scouting should be full of adventure as well as a school for extra wisdom a boy might not learn elsewhere.

Always, when Uncle Walton's Scouts weren't off camping or boating, they were deep into a service project. Himself was assistant Scout Master for a while and I'll never forget the time the Scouts came shouting for him in the middle of the night. They were calling out all hands to help look for a lost child. These guys were serious about their service.

This troop helped with Cub Scout projects, ushered at baseball games, and generally made themselves useful. Their willingness to serve was well known and they were asked to participate in all sorts of projects which needed the strength and energy of enthusiastic teenage boys.

Sooner or later, each succeeding group of Scouts found themselves at a Sunday morning worship service at camp. The topic was always, "Service Is The Rent You Pay For The Space You Occupy." Uncle Walton explained, in terms of God's will, the philosophy he had been leading the Scouts to follow. There is ample evidence that most of them never forgot it.

Although they were not privileged to be in Uncle Walton's Scout Troop, our two got the message about service. Berle worked on service projects with his own troop. Nancy served as a Youth Aide at the hospital and worked on projects with the church youth group.

One time, when Nancy's little ones were still in grammar school, I arrived for a visit to find them at their dining room table, diligently stuffing sandwiches and cookies into small paper bags.

"What are you doing?" I asked.

Lindsey smiled and popped a cookie into her mouth. "We're feeding the homeless," she mumbled through the cookie crumbs.

"And Lindsey," added Jason who had a few cookie crumbs on his chin as well. "Except she's not homeless—yet."

Lindsey rolled her eyes, her mouth too full of cookies for rebuttal.

"We're filling three hundred bags," added Jason, "and people from the church will take them to the homeless downtown."

I sampled a few cookies myself as I worked with them for almost two hours, filling lunch bags, serving others, feeling useful.

Not long after, I received a newspaper clipping featuring Berle's two sons, Nathan and Heath, in a story about their Cub Scout Pack gathering food for the homeless in Charlotte, North Carolina. "Good," I thought. "Start them early!"

Fortunate is the young person whose parents set an example of service to others. Children who watch their parents give a portion of their time to some good cause see that as a logical part of living. They are the ones who sign up for Scouts, the Red Cross Youth Program, church programs and school service clubs. Not only does this keep them out of trouble and provide an avenue for forming friendships, it teaches them the satisfaction of being useful.

Service to others is a sure cure for boredom. Any young person who shows signs of restlessness should be boosted, or booted, into a youth service organization—or challenged to go mow the neighbor's lawn.

She said she wanted to model in the fashion show...
He volunteered to be in the skiing contest...
Now they're not so sure...
But, people are depending on them.

What do you do?

He just knows he'll fail the exam...
She is sure the blind date will be awful...

How do you help?

Give them an attitude. It's called,

"FOR PITY'S SAKE, HAVE FUN!"

Watch them relax, enjoy, learn new skills and seek more adventures.

"If it's worth doing, it's worth messing up."
Uncle Jake

"For Pity's Sake, Have Fun"

Acting 102 was not my favorite course in college, mostly because of an uptight instructor who shouted, threatened and browbeat us during rehearsals, trying to get some sort of professional performance out of a bunch of giggling girls. By opening night we were thoroughly frightened of making the smallest mistake. Just before the play began, she would remind us, "I'll be out front listening to every word. If anything goes wrong I shall flunk you all!" Then she smiled and said, "For Pity's Sake, Have Fun!"

Naturally, we latched on to the phrase and, when exams loomed, or we were going on a blind date, we told each other, "For Pity's Sake, Have Fun."

During their growing up years, both our children managed to get themselves involved in an assortment of plays, concerts, parades and talent shows—the sort of thing for which you gleefully volunteer, diligently prepare, and then when the big moment comes, wonder what possessed you. We found "For Pity's Sake, Have Fun," murmured at the right moment, at least produced a rueful laugh. At best it helped provide a positive outlook on the ordeal ahead.

I remember one particular high school glee club concert. Nancy was enjoying the task of piano accompanist until, halfway through rehearsals, the director decided to add Handel's "Hallelujah Chorus" to the program. Nancy was aghast!

She started at once to practise the formidable accompaniment. "I'll never learn it in time," she groaned, her fingers stumbling again and again on a difficult passage. "Do you know how hard this is?" Her fist crashed on the keys.

"Sweetheart, that won't help," I said, secretly disgusted with the director. "Just give it your best shot."

Eventually she persuaded the director to let her play the right hand in the piece while the assistant accompanist played the left hand. They played well together at practise, but Nancy was still uneasy. Always a perfectionist, she dreaded this particular part of the performance and we knew it.

Just before the concert, I located her assistant and asked him to do me a favor. Although obviously puzzled by my request, he agreed to do it. As the director raised his baton for the "Hallelujah Chorus," the assistant leaned close to Nancy's ear and whispered, "For Pity's Sake, Have Fun." She smiled, relaxed, and made a small face in the direction of the audience, aimed, no doubt, at me. They sailed through the famous chorus without a hitch, and it was that moment which made the concert into a memory of triumph for Nancy—and me.

We found "For Pity's Sake, Have Fun" was wrong for trips to the dentist or the doctor, but worked well for exams, command visits with relatives, first dates, job hunting and anything involving an audience.

Many experiences in life may be faced with a mixture of anticipation and trepidation. I like to think an invitation to "Have Fun" in spite of the odds helped our children see how they might enjoy a situation instead of dreading it. Perhaps it gave them the nerve to try new experiences and accept new challenges.

Heroes are not made nor born.
They're carefully raised.
Most of them learn
Somewhere along the way,

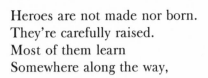

It's our job to help them discover, IT'S WORTH IT!

Jesus assures us, *"Blessed are you when people insult you, persecute you and falsely say all kinds of evil against you because of me."*

Matthew 5:11 NIV

"Sometimes Doing Right Gets You Into Trouble"

"Mother!" His feet were scarcely off the school bus. "Mother," he called.

"What is it, son?" I met him on the porch.

"I'm gonna get killed. I'm gonna die."

Seeing no guns, knives or pursing wildlife, I managed to stay calm.

"This guy, Joe, is gonna hit me with his cast. He already broke his hand on another kid he hit."

"That's why his hand's in a cast?"

He nodded. "Do you know how hard casts are? He'll kill me."

"Why you?" I asked.

"I told on him for smoking in the bathroom."

"Berle!" My children weren't raised to be tattletales.

"Well, Mother, the principal said I had to. He said if we saw someone smoking in the bathroom and didn't tell, we were as guilty as if we'd done it ourselves. He's gonna kill me. When he finds out, he'll hit me with that cast."

With an effort, I managed not to divulge my view of a principal who made unfair demands on conscientious children. Instead, I set out to soothe my son.

"He probably doesn't know you did it."

"He has to. I was the only one there except him and his friends."

"Well, son..." I took both his hands. "I'm going to do everything I can to see you don't get hurt, but this is as good a time as any for you to find out, Sometimes Doing Right Gets You Into Trouble. Look at what happened to Jesus! He did it right and they crucified him. Most people think it's worth it," I hastened to add.

Slightly mollified, he murmured, "I don't wanna get killed."

"I know," I said. "I think I can guarantee you won't."

This time there were no consequences. In our little chat, the principal assured me, "Most youngsters who smoke in the bathroom do so on a regular basis. They're unlikely to know who reported them."

The only time Berle did get into a fist fight was when another boy was picking on a small girl. Berle tried to make him quit, knowing it was the right thing to do. Fortunately, a teacher saw the whole thing and, when they were hauled off to the principal's office for fighting, she went along to explain.

"Punishment, or no punishment," Berle said, "I'd have done it again!"

Later, as a young Marine Lieutenant in charge of firing a twenty-one gun salute, using blanks in a seventy-five millimeter gun, Berle faced a more serious challenge. When time came to fire the gun during a practise, he noted that the street in front of the guns had not been cleared for safety's sake. Although he was firing blanks, the shock waves from the discharge could cause serious damage to the ears of people in the passing cars.

"Fire," ordered the Colonel in charge of the practise.

"Fire," repeated Berle's Captain.

"No, sir!" said Berle.

In the Marine Corps, refusing a direct order from a superior officer is not a small thing. Berle endured a thorough dressing down from the Colonel and a period of anxiety until the reason for his disobedience could be communicated to the irate man.

There's no way to put into words the satisfaction of "Doing Right" even if it gets you into trouble. It's one of those things you have to discover for yourself. Parents can only reassure their children they have found it so, hoping they, in turn, will have the courage to give it a try.

Saying things like:

"I'm gonna take my paper dolls and go home."

"I'll quit. They can't treat me that way."

"I'd rather stay home from the party than go in this old dress."

"She thinks she's better than me. I don't want to be on her team."

Leads to:

"If I can't be flower chairman, I'll quit the church."

"The other guy got a raise and I didn't. They can have this job."

"If she won't let me have my way, I'll get a divorce."

Grandma always said:

"DON'T CUT OFF YOUR NOSE TO SPITE YOUR FACE"

It's *always* a mistake to give up something you want, just to get even. That's called "cutting off your nose to spite your face."

"He who leaves in a huff leaves only puff behind."

Fortune Cookie

"Don't Cut Off Your Nose To Spite Your Face"

Slowly I walked down the steps, my chin held high, careful not to show my anger. Finally in my car, I slammed it into gear. "How dare she!" I thought. For two years I had served my time as assistant Scout leader, following the ideas and suggestions—sometimes orders—of the leader, never allowed to try out ideas of my own. Now she was gone. It was surely my turn to be leader. But no, the Troop Organizer had introduced me to Mrs. Snelley, just moved to town, practically a professional Scout with dozens of training programs to her credit.

"I won't do it!" I thought furiously. "They can just find another toady to do this woman's bidding. I'll show them they can't push me around." I thought of how the girls would miss me, how much I would miss them. I began to create a fantasy. The Scouts would rebel against my going. I pictured the picket signs they would use, demanding my return. Then, out of the past came Mother's reminder, flung across my jumbled thoughts like a bright banner: "Don't Cut Off Your Nose To Spite Your Face."

I realized I would miss the Scouts' gay laughter and funny jokes. What would shy little Marie do if I wasn't there to help her reach out to the other girls? What about the new songs I was teaching them? Could this new leader carry a tune?

I doubt it, I thought resentfully. Realizing I would lose more than I would gain by quitting, I decided to accept the new leader.

She was wonderful, listening to my ideas, giving me the advantage of her years of training and becoming my very good friend.

Thankful my mother taught me, "Don't Cut Off Your Nose To Spite Your Face," I have watched grown-ups do incredible things to themselves. A newlywed friend, living on a low income, deliberately scorched her husband's good shirt, because it was a gift from an old girlfriend. Another friend quit her tennis team. A newcomer hurt her feelings, so she gave up healthy exercise and long-term friendships she had enjoyed for years. My gifted Sunday School teacher resigned. Someone suggested her lessons were running too long.

Watching these people unnecessarily deprive themselves of a lot of satisfaction for no good reason, I determined to teach our children, "Don't Cut Off Your Nose To Spite Your Face."

Human nature being what it is, I didn't have long to wait. Nancy was still in Grammar School the day she settled down to the kitchen table with a discouraged air.

"Mom, I'm not going to work on that art project any more," she said. "Sarah changes everything I do and criticizes everything she doesn't change."

"How can she get away with that?" I asked.

"She's teacher's pet and Mrs. Jones thinks she can do no wrong. The project's going to look just awful. I don't want to have anything to do with it."

"But if you drop out, you won't get to enter your own project in the competition, will you?"

"I don't care," she said. "They can try to win without me."

"Wow, it sounds to me like you're going to Cut Off Your Nose To Spite Your Face."

"What's that supposed to mean?" She frowned at me, not sure she wanted to know.

"Think about it," I said.

The next morning she was her usual, bouncy self. "I've decided I'm going to simply ignore Sarah and do my part of the project the way I want to," she said. "And, if I get a chance, I'll fix some of her messy work. I can't let the rest of the committee down. I'll at least get to enter my project and, if the other entries are worse than ours…"

"Nancy!"

"Well, they could be. All the committees could have a 'Sarah.' And we might win."

I gave her a hug. "It sounds to me like you're not going to Cut Off Your Nose To Spite Your Face, after all," I said.

"Whatever that means!" responded my sassy daughter.

Somebody has to set the rules or we would have chaos.

Children work best when they know what the rules are.

So do adults.

Although rebellion is sometimes appropriate and justice is sometimes not served, effective adults know one thing for sure about people in authority:

"THEY'RE NOT RUNNING A POPULARITY CONTEST"

If kids respect authority, they spend—
- more time learning,
  and less time resenting.
- more time accomplishing,
  and less time complaining.

St. Paul wrote, *"Do you want to be free from fear of the one in authority? Then do what is right and he will commend you."*

Romans 13:3 NIV

"They're Not Running A Popularity Contest"

In my high school class, there was a boy whose parents thought he could do no wrong. In fact, if anyone indicated otherwise, they made a big issue of it, loudly protesting his innocence, vigorously accusing teachers, principals, students and even police officers of misjudging their perfect son. In those days you didn't hear as much about "demanding my rights," nor did parents sue at the drop of a hat, but it was approximately the same thing.

So far as I know, this "perfect" soul was the only member of our high school class who wound up in jail. His classmates were not surprised. Too often we watched this young man insist on his version of an incident, then stand by and witness his parents berate someone in authority on his behalf. He was raised to believe he was always right, no matter what he did. What his parents didn't teach him, society had to. The hard way!

Of course parents should protect their children from real abuse, or misuse, by anyone. On the other hand, the little injustices, real or imagined, can be handled with, "They're Not Running A Popularity Contest." I suspect this is a Marine Corps "saying."

My daddy, who was Air Force, put it another way.

"I can't stand my teacher. She is so dull and boring," I said.

"Do your classmates like her?" he asked.

"I guess so!"

"Then there can't be too much wrong with the teacher, can there? Best you figure out how to get along with her, whether you like her or not."

You can't run a good military organization without respect for authority. Neither can you run an effective school, nor a worthwhile society.

When Nancy or Berle complained about their teachers, Scout leaders or Sunday School teachers, we listened carefully for any real injustice. Hearing none (and we seldom did), we usually said, "Your Teacher's Not Running A Popularity Contest, you know. He doesn't have to get along with you. You have to get along with him."

This worked well for those times when we, too, stood accused by our kids. "Dad, you're so unfair. I promised the guys I'd go on this trip and now you won't let me. You're mean!"

"Maybe so," his father would say, "but I'm in charge here and I'm Not Running A Popularity Contest. Three nine-year-olds can't spend a weekend in those woods without an adult along."

I confess, while I agreed with "They're Not Running A Popularity Contest," I was more prone to negotiate.

"I've washed the dog three times in a row, now," said young son. "Why isn't it Nancy's turn? You're not fair!"

Instead of "I'm Not running A Popularity Contest," I found myself saying, "I didn't mean to be dogmatic about your washing the dog. Would it help if we both pitched in?"

"Maybe!" He carefully examined his shoes, not meeting my eyes. "I said you were unfair, not dogma ... what was that again?"

"Dogmatic! It means stubborn and unyielding."

Their father taught them respect for authority. I taught vocabulary. In the long run, it made no difference. They had to respect me. After all, I was the cook and chauffeur. Besides, the quickest way to arouse their father's ire was to be disrespectful to their mother.

At home I backed up Himself with, "Your Teacher Is Not Running A Popularity Contest." When I went to school, as I often did, my inner thoughts were, "Hey, lady, I'm on his side. What are you doing here to my kid?" Severely quelling my maternal instinct, I tried to act as intermediary rather than antagonist, looking for a better understanding between our children and people in authority.

When Berle was a third-grader, he was assigned to fourth grade for math and science. It was one of those experimental programs the schools are always trying, and I found myself called to school by the fourth grade teacher.

"Berle always sits in the back of the room, and often doesn't get his homework," she told me. "I am disappointed in his work. I know he can do better."

I took a deep breath. "Please take a look in your roll book and check his age," I said. "You'll find he is young for third grade, much less fourth. He may be big for his age, but the older boys intimidate him. They tell him he has to sit in the back because he's a third-grader. Sometimes he doesn't hear the homework assignment and he said you told the class not to ask you to repeat it."

She was astonished. "That was only one day. The class was noisy and inattentive. I didn't mean he could never ask me to repeat it. You must think I'm a terrible teacher."

"Not at all!" I managed a smile. "I know my son tends to be a bit literal minded."

She returned my smile. "Tell Berle my orders are for him to sit in the front row from now on—and he can tell that to the fourth-graders. Tell him if he'll wait until after class I'll repeat the homework assignments if he needs them. Maybe the fourth-graders don't need to hear that," she added as an afterthought.

In less than a month, she was his favorite teacher and I think it was mutual. At any rate, I learned a little Mama Mediation can often smooth the way at school.

All these years, Berle has remembered this slogan. Recently he checked in with us after a week at Scout Camp, spent supervising eleven lively youngsters. "We got a lot done," he said. "Every Scout completed at least three merit badge requirements. We had a great time, probably because I Didn't Run A Popularity Contest."

Sometimes the battle's lost before it starts.
Sometimes there's nothing they can do about it.
Sometimes there's nothing you can do about it.
Sometimes there's nothing *anyone* can do about it.

What will you do?

Sympathize; help them feel sorry for themselves?
Tell them how badly life is treating them?
Accept the fact that it's going to make them miserable?
Listen to their constant complaints?

Or, suggest they learn to —

"COOPERATE WITH THE INEVITABLE"

Accept what has happened.
Find a way to be productive in spite of it.
Keep cheerful, regardless.
Look for ways to make the best of it.

St. Francis of Assisi put it more eloquently:
"God, grant me the serenity to accept the things I cannot change, the courage to change the things I can, and the wisdom to know the difference."

"Cooperate With The Inevitable"

Minnie Johnson was cook and confidant for my great-grandmother Alice Hitch. At the turn of the century, they lived a few blocks apart in Waycross, Georgia. Grandmother Hitch lived in a large house downtown, Minnie in a little one on the outskirts of town with her husband who was an invalid, her son who was an alcoholic, and her daughter who was always having babies. Minnie's other son was in jail. All of them depended on Minnie for...everything! Still, Minnie always sang as she worked. With Minnie in the kitchen, the sound of Gospel hymns, sung with obvious enthusiasm, mingled with the aroma of fried chicken, fresh cooked corn and home made biscuits pervading great-grandmother's house. Or so my grandma told me.

Knowing most of the troubles that Minnie endured, great-grandmother asked her one day, "Minnie, with all the burdens you are carrying, how can you sing so joyously?"

"Well, Miss Alice," she said, "after all these years I've just learned to Cooperate With The Inevitable."

When life gets challenging, it doesn't take long to discover who does, or doesn't Cooperate With The Inevitable.

I learned the hard way. Himself and I had been married only a short time when the Marine Corps decided he was needed in Japan for a year. I wasn't invited! The Marine Corps said so. That left me nothing to do but "Cooperate With The Inevitable," taking my pregnant self home to Mother and Daddy while the man I had promised to love and cherish went so far away I was barely able to correspond with him. I had two choices: I could make the best of it, as cheerfully as possible, or be miserable and a burden to others. Like Minnie, I found it helped to sing a lot.

Later, when Nancy complained about missing an outing with her friends because we had planned a family camping trip, I suggested she "Cooperate With The Inevitable." We felt she would look back, some day, and know that family time is important, too. Meantime, she needed to get over her disappointment and enjoy our family outing.

When Berle bemoaned the fact that we were moving again, leaving behind his friends and his carefully worked out strategy to be drum major of the band the following year, I shared his pain. After giving him some sympathy, I suggested he "Cooperate With The Inevitable" and try to look forward to new friends and new adventures. "Maybe your new school will have a band that needs a well-trained drum major," I added, hoping this was so. (Actually, it turned out to be a bigger and better band, and he enjoyed the challenge.)

When we moved to Clearwater Beach between his sophomore and junior years at high school, we promised him a ski boat to ease the pain of leaving his friends. Boats were more costly than we had planned and we had to renege on the promise, feeling terrible about it. Cooperating With The Inevitable, he comforted me, "It's all right, Mom. I'm a big boy. I can do without it. There are lots of other ways to entertain myself."

To my delight, he soon found a friend who needed a place to store his ski boat. It fitted well in our back yard, just three blocks from a launch ramp, and the two boys spent happy hours skiing together. Berle couldn't have enjoyed the boat more if it were his.

Sometimes we used this slogan for less serious things. When Berle got grouchy on a long trip, Nancy could be heard to murmur that he wasn't Cooperating With The Inevitable very well. "I'll cooperate you," he would say and the ensuing tussle signaled a need for a short stop to "run down the street and back, you rowdy kids."

Just once, Berle had the temerity to use it when he came home late from a date. Finding his father waiting up to explain to him the error of his ways, he ventured, "Dad, you know I'm always late. Can't you learn to Cooperate With The Inevitable?"

"No!"

Somehow that ended the conversation.

We don't believe in simply letting life roll over you when there are ways to fight back, but sometimes there's no choice. We tried to help our children recognize the difference.

"If there's a way out," we told them, "you need to look for it. If there isn't, it's best to Cooperate With The Inevitable as cheerfully and productively as possible."

It's a short step from—

"There's a spot on this apple; I don't want it."
    to:
"My wife has a fault; I'm leaving her."

"I came in second; I'm a lousy ball player."
    to:
"I got turned down twice; I can't get a job."

"I wanted a new bike, not this second-hand one."
    to:
"All we can afford is this crummy house."

Help them learn to look at the positive and the possibilities.

It's no fun to be —

"A HOLE-IN-THE-DONUT PERSON"

"The world is so full of a number of things,"
said Grandma, *"I'm sure we should all be as
happy as kings."*

"Don't Be A Hole In The Donut Person"

"Oh, don't bother about him," said my daddy. "He's a Hole In The Donut Person anyway."

"Hole In The Donut?"

"Yes, you know:

> 'As you wander on through life, my dear,
> Whatever be your goal,
> Keep your eye upon the donut
> And not upon the hole.'"

"Oh, I see!"

But I didn't! It was years before I discovered there are people who only look at what's missing. They see the glass as half empty instead of half full. The raise is long overdue instead of an improvement in the paycheck. Dinner out was spoiled because the coffee wasn't hot enough. The sugary deliciousness of the donut is diminished because the hole looks so big.

In short, the Hole In The Donut Person is so busy thinking about what he doesn't have that he doesn't appreciate what he has. He misses the small joys and delights that make life more fun than trouble. He doesn't even appreciate his own accomplishments. He also misses out on some happy friendships. Who wants to be around a Hole In The Donut Person anyway?

They start early! "Mother, I don't want this cookie."

"Why not, Honey? Mine is delicious."

"Yes, but mine has a crumble on the side. I wonder if a bug ate some of it. Ugh!"

Or, "I'm not going to Mary's party."

"Didn't you get an invitation?"

"Yes, but everyone else got theirs yesterday and mine didn't come until today."

Don't laugh! I've known adults who say things like, "I'm not going to that church any more. The preacher never has time to shake my hand."

Just to show how common this is with kids, Rick Morgan, a clever young man who works with pre-school children, wrote a charming little ditty, recorded by Dulcimer Dan of Raleigh, North Carolina. "My Raisin Has A Wrinkle," complains the vocalist, "My banana has a spot...." Doesn't that sound familiar?

Nancy was bitterly disappointed when she failed to win a scholarship for a summer music program. She was one of three selected from her school to compete for it and we felt it was an honor just to be selected. When it looked as though the disappointment might spoil her whole summer, we suggested she not be a Hole In The Donut Person about it. She thought it over and promptly found a summer job in her favorite ceramic shop.

In third grade, Berle was one of five students asked to play the Flutaphone in a class concert. As practice progressed, the other four dropped out, leaving him playing a solo. When his big moment came, the teacher accompanied him at a tempo that left me breathless, just listening. I was amazed that he managed to keep up, missing only one note. As the audience and his classmates applauded enthusiastically, he stepped back into line and commented to the girl beside him, "I messed up!"

"Whoa!" I told him later. "That's a Hole In The Donut attitude. You were the only one who even tried. You did a marvelous job and everybody was pleased and excited. Not even dozens of missed notes should make you feel like a failure."

Regardless of outward circumstances, the little things in a personality make the difference between a generally happy life and disgruntlement. Happy people are welcome wherever they go. People who have a Hole In The Donut personality are only tolerated. We felt Daddy's injunction, "Don't Be A Hole In The Donut Person," was well worth passing along.

Success in life, in business, in marriage,
in self-approval, and in relationships,
awaits the person who learns early how to

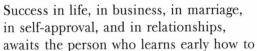

"GO THE EXTRA MILE"

It pays to:
- Find and repair the reasons a friend is angry,
- Search for ways to be more useful at work,
- Do more than is expected of you at school,
- Never "count favors" at home.

Teach them early to be an "Extra-miler."

"If someone forces you to go one mile, go with
him two miles."

Matthew 5:41

"Go The Extra Mile"

In the days when the Romans were hated rulers in Palestine there was a law, bitterly resented by the Jewish people. Under this law, any Roman soldier could require a civilian to escort him for a mile on his journey, probably carrying his load. How hateful to be interrupted in the midst of a task and required to walk a long distance with a stranger whose power over you is bitterly resented. The Bible reports that Jesus told his followers, "If someone requires you to go a mile with him, go two." Hearing this, they must have wondered whose side He was on.

"Go the first mile," he could have explained, "because you have to. Go the second to show God's love."

Imagine a young Roman soldier, hot, tired, lonely and perhaps a bit homesick. Picture his surprise and curiosity when a follower of Jesus finished the required first mile, shifted the soldier's load to his other shoulder and prepared to walk with him an extra mile, smiling as he went.

Taught early, children take well to being what we call "extra-milers." It fits their generous natures.

"Mother, Jimmy took my bat!"

"Well, give him your ball. He can't play soft ball with just a bat. Go The Extra Mile!"

"You're kidding!"

"No, I'm not. Try it!"

With luck, Jimmy and Berle wind up in a friendly game of ball, instead of a tug of war over a bat.

"Mother, I've called Marie three times to try and plan the class party. She keeps disagreeing with me and slamming down the phone."

"Well, Go The Extra Mile! This time, start by agreeing with one of her ideas ...."

"I've already done that."

"Well, agree with another. Then slip yours in when she's not looking."

Whether Nancy and Marie wind up agreeing or not, Nancy has the satisfaction of knowing she "went the extra mile" to make it work.

Better still, if they complain that Daddy, or Mother, or a teacher is demanding too much, that line about the extra mile comes in handy.

I don't know if our Lord intended it to be used that way, but harried parents need all the help they can get.

Of course, there was the time Nancy complained her teacher was piling on the homework. I suggested she "Go The Extra Mile" by doing some unrequired extra work for class. This netted me an indignant sniff. But she quit complaining.

"Go The Extra Mile" has always seemed to me good marriage insurance. It's not the fifty/fifty marriages (or other friendships) that work. Success in relationships calls for at least seventy-five percent from each partner. Come to think of it, it takes a lot of people regularly going the Extra Mile, above and beyond the call of duty, to make the world a fit place in which to live.

There's a reward for "extra-milers." It's called satisfaction!

After the automobile accident...
After the first job failure...
After the end of a big romance...
After she's lost the scholarship...

... is not the time to tell them,

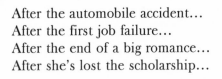

By then it's too late! Better to harass them as youngsters with:

- "Do it right the first time..."
- "Start early..."
- "Take your time..."
- "Give yourself plenty of time..."

Why? Because "haste makes waste!"

Or, as is said in Proverbs, *"The plans of the diligent lead to profit as surely as haste leads to poverty."*

Proverbs 2:15 NIV

"Haste Makes Waste"

We were halfway to her music teacher's house when Nancy discovered she had the wrong music. "For pity's sakes, Nancy, you know what time your lesson is. Why don't you have all your music together?" I barely controlled my exasperation. Each minute with a music teacher is expensive, whether you're on time or not.

"Haven't you learned, Haste Makes Waste?" I added.

"I wouldn't have forgotten if you hadn't rushed me, Mother."

Her sassy comeback made me think. What do you do with a mother who's so overscheduled she's forever rushing around and demanding that you hurry, only to tell you, "Haste Makes Waste?"

Next music lesson, I did it differently. "It's thirty minutes until we leave for your music lesson," I cautioned her. "Remember, Haste Makes Waste. Please get your music together now, so we won't have to hurry."

"I've already done it," she said with exaggerated patience. As usual, she was way ahead of me when it came to being organized.

What's a parent to do? The same kid who can chase wildly across the yard after his dog, or a friend, or nothing at all, will take at least ten minutes to move from the door of the house to the door of the car—especially if you're in a hurry. My grandmother always told us, "Haste Makes Waste." At least once a week I am aware of the truth of this statement. As a mother who often makes three false starts before I get out of the driveway, teaching my children "Haste Makes Waste" was difficult.

But I tried! After all—Grandma said it.

Nancy hurries through a sewing project because it's overdue and, guess what, she does it wrong and it has to be ripped out. "Next time, remember, Haste Makes Waste," I suggest as I start ripping on one end while she does the other.

Berle rushes through mowing the lawn because it's a boring task. He wants to get it over with. "Haste Makes Waste," I warn him. Sure enough, his dad points out all the spots he missed, and bids him do it again.

I insist we hurry with the dishes so we won't be late to the movie. Soapy hands slip, and a treasured pitcher crashes to the floor. Seeing my distress, no one mentions, "Haste Makes Waste!" They don't have to. I know!

I thought about giving up on this particular slogan. Children have a way of communicating, "What you do speaks so loud I don't hear what you say," even when they don't say it. But a look down the years suggests more terrible consequences of haste than a broken pitcher. If, when they are little, they don't learn to start early so they need not choose between being late, or getting in a rush, they're liable to decide the speed limit isn't important when they are old enough to drive. That can lead to speeding tickets, or destruction of life and limb. If they don't learn to do a job right the first time in grammar school, what employer is going to allow them to waste his time getting it right when they're adults? If they are not taught by their parents to slow down, take a deep breath and think about what they're doing, who's going to teach them? Too many people learn that Haste Makes Waste after a terrible tragedy.

I decided we'd better keep this one. Wandering down the hall, I found Berle happily cleaning his room by pushing certain items under his bed instead of putting them where they belonged.

"In a hurry, son?" My question was all innocence.

"No, Ma'am!" He gave me a wary look. "Just taking a short cut. I wanna go to Jerry's before supper."

"And when do you plan to undo your short cut?" I asked.

"Well..." He started pulling items from under the bed and putting them away.

I stooped to help him, ignoring the chores waiting for my attention. The most terrible waste, after all, is not really haste, but missing times to be with your children while they are still with you.

"Thanks, Mother!" He brushed my cheek with a kiss as, his task complete, he hurried out the door.

"For helping you clean up?"

"No," he tossed over his shoulder. "For not telling me Haste Makes Waste."

The more you know about your kids,
The more you can do for them.
The more they tell you what's in their hearts,
The better you can understand.
If you listen when they need to talk,
They'll talk when you need to hear.

Don't leave it to chance.

Find opportunities to show them that

"IT PAYS TO COMMUNICATE"

Have them say it out loud: "It pays to communicate!"

Do it when they're young. When they're older, you'll be glad you did.

"Tell me your heart, that I might love you more."
Author unknown

"It Pays To Communicate"

"Mo-o-o-other!" Nancy came sobbing into the house, followed closely by a youngster from the neighborhood, a little older and slightly bigger than our little girl. He was in second grade; Nancy was a brand new first-grader.

"Mrs. Garris…" His small figure was stiff, his voice stern. "Nancy pushed me."

"No-o-o!" Nancy clutched me around the knees.

"What did you do to her, young man?" I was immediately defensive of my suffering child.

"Nothing!"

"Are you sure?"

"Sure. I was leaning over to tie my shoe and she just came up and shoved me. I hurt my nose." He showed me a minuscule scratch.

"Let me guess. Your name is Bertram."

"How'd you know?"

Easy! Nancy had complained for two weeks about "Bertram" who kept pushing and shoving her on the way to school. Dismayed because I could no longer be on hand to protect her from bullies, I had instructed her, for the first time, "Fight back, Honey. Just push him back, hard! You can do it."

She wouldn't deny she had pushed him. Obviously she had, but couldn't find the words to explain. My dainty daughter, too timid to defend herself directly, had waited until his back was turned and pushed him over on his nose.

I tried not to smile.

Sensing I was not going to punish her to his satisfaction, he jutted out his small chin. "I guess I'll just have to report this to the principal!"

Nancy clutched me tighter, her sobs increasing. Momentarily dismayed, I pictured my small daughter, accused before a principal who wouldn't understand. Then I realized the principal probably knew Bertram very well and would, no doubt, have a clear picture of what had happened.

"Bertram, you need to learn not to pester people if you don't want to be pestered." I said it as gently as I could with my daughter sobbing in my arms. "If you leave Nancy alone, she'll leave you alone. Now run along."

With a damp washcloth smoothing her tears away, Nancy leaned against my knee. "He's so mean. How did you know?" she murmured.

I didn't want to miss the chance.

"I knew, Honey, because you had told me all about him, and the principal will know, too. I'm sure others have told her. Remember It Pays To Communicate."

"I know," she said.

Not communicating can actually be hazardous. In eighth grade, Berle went from his middle school to the high school for band practice. As boys will, he and his friends took a shortcut through a wooded area, rather than the long way around by pavement.

"Mother," he said one day after school, "there was a big boy on the path today. He was smoking a cigarette and talking to me. When we saw someone coming, he handed me his cigarette and asked me to hold it for him."

"Did you?"

"Well, yes. He just put it in my hand and I hated to drop a lit cigarette in the woods. It was kinda funny looking with a strange odor."

"Could it have been marijuana?" I tried to sound calm.

"Is that how they do marijuana? In cigarettes?"

"From what I've heard."

"Then I don't hold anybody's cigarettes for them, right?"

"Better still," I said, "you stay away from young people who are smoking ... anything! Do you know what happens if you get caught with a marijuana cigarette?"

"I'm accused of drug possession."

"And it would be your word against his."

"Whooeee!"

"Right!"

Aboard a military base, if a student is found with drugs in his possession, the family is moved out of military housing—immediately—and left to find suitable, usually more expensive quarters elsewhere.

I took his face between my hands. "Thank God you told me."

"Yes'm," he said meekly. "You always said It Pays To Communicate."

It always upsets me to see children trying to talk to parents who are not listening. It happens all the time. Just look around you. It's amazing how many people live together, each not knowing what the other is thinking. Communication is a skill that must be taught, preferably by example.

We found ourselves with two deliberate "listening times." At supper, we developed the habit of talking about the events of the day. If the grown-ups got off on serious subjects before the children had their turn, Nancy would say, "Wait, Mother, you haven't heard about my day's adventures."

It became a competition to see who could tell the funniest story of the day. Supper conversation was expected to be pleasant, quarrels and complaints saved until later.

At bedtime we "tucked them in." When they were little, we heard their prayers, or prayed with them before we kissed them goodnight. As they got old enough to "say my own prayers, thank you," we spent a few minutes chatting. This was the time to discover what was in their hearts and minds, a time for confessions (from both parent and child), for talking about the hurts and worries that make life miserable.

Sharing what's going on in their lives when they are little is a habit that pays off when they are older. It leaves open a door in the wall teenagers tend to build around themselves.

Nancy was a freshman in high school when she came to me with a big, thick book. "Do I have to read this?" she asked. "Our English Lit teacher assigned it."

To my surprise, it was a satire on the military system and the men in it. The chaplain was depicted as a coward and a charlatan. The men were either stupid or dishonest. I opened the book at random and came upon a section which graphically described the hero's dealings with a prostitute he despised.

I was appalled! The books I read as I grew up had a large influence on my life. Some people may simply read books. I have always "experienced" them. This was not the sort of experience my daughter ever needed to know about, much less have forced on her at the age of fifteen.

The principal was reluctantly cooperative when I informed him that Nancy was not going to read the book and she was assigned another book, less destructive of her innocence. Thank goodness she knew It Pays To Communicate.

If you expect them to be on their own at a reasonable age, they need to learn responsibility.

If they learn early to:
- Pick up their clothes,
- Run errands,
- Be Mother's or Daddy's big helper...

...then they'll understand when you tell them,

"I EXPECT YOU TO BE PART OF THE SOLUTION, NOT PART OF THE PROBLEM"

This is a good answer to:
- "Why can't I drop out of school?"
- "Whaddaya mean I'm too young to drink?"
- "It's my money; I'll do as I please with it!"
- "Who cares...."

"A foolish son brings grief to his father and bitterness to the one who bore him."
Proverbs 17:25 NIV

"I Expect You To Be Part Of The Solution— Not Part Of The Problem"

There are a thousand ways a child can bring joy into the lives of parents. There are also a thousand ways children can break your heart by becoming Part Of The Problem. Runaways, alcoholics, drug addicts, unwed parents, self-centered people—all those who are unwilling or unable to be a Part Of The Solution in society remain Part Of The Problem.

I acknowledge that some of these people did not "bring it on themselves." I also insist that parents can do everything right and still have children who are Part Of The Problem. The human mind and spirit are too complex for parents to have any guarantees.

Nevertheless, parents need to try.

I read somewhere that a way to avoid juvenile delinquency is to give children responsibilities in the home.

"Assigned chores," wrote the author, "help children feel important and necessary to the family." He bewailed the demise of coal scuttles and butter churns, not to mention chicken feeding and egg gathering, all chores which kept children usefully occupied as well as physically active. With this in mind, we made it a point to give our children tasks they could handle as early as possible.

It helps, I discovered, if parents are a shade too lazy to take over the kid's chores except on rare occasions, and just sloppy enough to be pleased with less than perfect results. Lavish praise, willingly bestowed, is also helpful if you want them to be Part Of The Solution.

When it came to questions about drinking, smoking, drugs, unwed parenting, laziness and other damaging habits, we didn't hesitate to explain things clearly to Nancy and Berle. "The answer is no," we often said, "because We Expect You To Be A Part Of The Solution, Not A Part Of The Problem."

We never believed the parenting myth: "No matter what you say, they're going to try it for themselves."

This came up in a conversation with two good friends. They insisted all kids tried drugs, whether their parents had warned them against them or not. Although I believed in my heart that my children had never tried drugs, I didn't argue. It was my word against theirs.

When I told Nancy about it, she was indignant. "Mother," she said, "I've never tried drugs and I never intend to. You should have defended me." She gave me a saucy smile. "Besides, if I get all messed up with drugs, how can I be Part Of The Solution?"

We never agreed with that other myth, "If you tell them not to do it, it just makes them want to try it."

Himself was very clear about this one. "It's our responsibility to make sure they know the possible consequences of their actions," he said. "If they do it anyway, we stand by to pick up the pieces, but the results are on their shoulders, and they know it."

When Berle was a junior in high school, he discovered the excitement of computers. He missed classes, working on computer projects. Girl friends waited impatiently as he talked computer with their fathers. Work took second place while he lingered at school with his new interest. I think he even missed a couple of skiing trips.

One day, as I drove him home from school, he was explaining to me the day's computer assignment, using not one word I could understand. He found it exhilarating. I saw my opportunity.

"You sound like I feel when I've written an editorial that's clear and precise with every word exactly right," I said. "It's so neat when your mind is clicking on all cylinders, isn't it?"

"Yeah!" His mood was jubilant.

"Can you imagine anyone wanting to put something in their bodies that would muddy their brains and spoil that?"

"I hadn't thought about it like that," he said, "but you're right. Mom, you know I'm never going to mess with drugs. As many times as you have told me I've got to be Part Of The Solution, how can I do drugs?"

He returned to his recital of the joys of programming computers. I still didn't understand what he was talking about.

Kids need idle time for day dreaming — and planning their future. BUT....

He spends long hours glued to the television set, watching whatever comes along.

She goes to her room and, stretched across the bed, listens by the hour to lyrics of modern songs, lyrics that produce emotions she's not yet ready for.

You wonder what to do.

You're the parent here so it's your job to:
- Dig them out
- Turn off the TV
- Unplug the boom box

Tell them...

"SATAN WILL FIND SOME MISCHIEF YET FOR IDLE HANDS TO DO"

Find them a hobby — any hobby. Offer a challenge — any challenge. Assign them a chore — any chore.

Nobody wants a lazy wife, husband, boss, employee, son or daughter.

In the letter to the Thessalonians we read, *"We hear that some among you are idle. They are not busy, they are busybodies. Such people we command and urge in the Lord Jesus Christ to settle down and earn the bread they eat."*
2 Thessalonians 3:11-12 NIV

"Satan Will Find Some Mischief Yet For Idle Hands To Do"

Having spent many pleasant hours sitting idly by the Gulf of Mexico, looking for special treasures in a mound of tiny sea shells, or gazing endlessly over the sparkling waves, with no particular thoughts in mind, I have a hard time distinguishing between "creative thinking time" and idleness. Perhaps it's just as well my Grandmother frequently reminded me, "Satan Will Find Some Mischief Yet For Idle Hands To Do."

Finding me in the kitchen, a half-washed dish in my hand, the dish rag poised in midair as my thoughts winged far away, she applied this slogan liberally. Looking back, I'm sure her exasperation had as much to do with concern for my future as for the unwashed dishes. All the experts are now saying what Grandmother already knew—children must be given their own responsibilities as early as possible if they are to grow up to be self-motivated, useful citizens.

What's a mother to do? No one wants their children to be those "Type A" personalities, pushing themselves unmercifully whether there's a need or not, winding up with heart attacks or nervous breakdowns. Neither do you want them to spend their lives in lazy idleness.

Like Grandma, I preferred to err on the side of keeping the kids as busy as possible. They could daydream all they liked if I wasn't watching or was distracted myself. (Mothers don't daydream, you understand, they "distract.") But let them spend too much time in front of the TV, or in teasing one another, and I didn't hesitate to instruct them, "Satan Will Find Some Mischief Yet For Idle Hands To Do," adding, "Get those hands busy! Go practice!"

My theory is there's no such thing as too much piano practice, unless, of course, Dad's favorite TV show is on.

Unfortunately, modern mothers must decide which TV moments are "idle time" and which aren't. Our Nancy is very firm about this. When she decides the one-eyed monster is wasting her children's time, she flips the off switch and says, "Let's turn off the TV and have some fun."

I knew I was in no danger of raising "Type A's" when Berle complained, "Mother, I wasn't being idle. That was creative contemplating."

"I'll creative contemplate you," I told him, "if you don't get your sassy self in there and do the laundry."

Nancy went about her business so quietly it was hard to know when she was idle. I never worried about her after friends reported on an overnight trip she took with her church group.

"We couldn't believe it," said Sue. "We had only a few minutes in the motel room before our appointment and everybody else was lounging on the bed, or in a chair. Not Nancy! She took some dress material out of her suitcase and started pinning a pattern to it. It was half cut out before we had to leave."

Berle was another matter. He was always either full speed ahead, or stretched out in some comfortable place with his eyes closed. By his senior year, he was involved in so many activities I worried that he was overdoing it, until the day I passed one of his classmates leaning against a corner light pole and staring off into space. He might have been waiting for the bus, but I knew this young man had been in trouble and it seemed to me that, standing there, he could pose for a poster with the title, "Satan Will Find Some Mischief Yet For Idle Hands To Do."

Arriving home, I found our son in his room, practicing for the upcoming drum major tryouts. "Are you sure you have enough to do?" I asked. "Are you staying busy enough?"

"Mother," he said, "come sit down a minute. Is the heat getting you? Let me get you a drink of water. You need to slow down a bit. Try a little idleness," he added. "I'll hold Satan at bay while you do."

"That's my sweater. Who said you could wear it?"

"Hey, you wore my slacks last week."

"But I asked you! Why are you always stealing my things?"

OR...

"That's my sweater. Who said you could wear it?"

"Oh, I'm sorry. I didn't think you'd care. I'll put it back."

"No, that's all right. Next time ask, okay?"

When you get into an argument and you want to win ... or, if you want to keep a friendship in spite of an argument, remember that

"A SOFT ANSWER TURNS AWAY WRATH"

It's the quickest way to stop an argument. It leaves your opponent confused and feeling guilty. It keeps you from saying things you'll regret. Best of all, it lets you be the good guy in the situation.

Or, as we read in Proverbs, *"A gentle answer turns away wrath, but a harsh word stirs up anger."*

Proverbs 15:1 NIV

"A Soft Answer Turns Away Wrath"

"What's the matter, son? Why so glum?" His dinner was untouched, an event so rare it called for thermometers and health questions.

"It's nothing, Mother. Just something Joe said."

"How about telling me what it was?"

His eyes filled with tears. "He said my daddy was gonna be killed in Vietnam and I'd never see him again."

"Honey, what a stupid thing for him to say." Berle was only seven and missing his father badly. I held him close while I controlled my own tears, unable to believe the cruelty of his favorite playmate.

"Sweetie, Daddy's not going to get killed in Vietnam. He's not even going to get hurt. He's going to be safely home in another six months." For my own sake, as well as his, I had to believe this was so.

"Well," he said, "Joe's daddy is a plumber, and I told him his daddy was going to get caught in a Johnny and flush himself down the drain and drown."

My anguish and sympathy evaporated. These two deserved each other. What a pair!

"It sounds to me like the two of you are about even," I said. "Why don't you go apologize to him for saying such a horrid thing about his daddy, and ask him to go for a bike ride?"

"Me apologize? He started it." He was indignant.

"What difference does it make? Is he angry with you?"

"Yeah! I made him cry."

"Son, he's your friend. Don't you know A Soft Answer Turns Away Wrath?"

"Even when he says something awful like that?"

"Yes!" I handed him the hot dog off his plate and nudged him towards the door.

Halfway there, he turned back. "Mother, what would you have said?"

For a moment I was stymied. Berle's reaction was perfectly normal for a seven-year-old. Was I asking too much to expect him to apologize? Well, Mothers should finish what they start.

"I don't blame you for saying what you did, Berle. I just hate to see a good friendship wasted over two stupid remarks."

"But what would you have said?"

"I hope something like, 'Joe, don't talk that way about my daddy. You wouldn't want me to say your daddy was going to die, would you?' I know that's hard to do, but it's important."

I wasn't privy to the resultant conversation between the boys, but the friendship was restored and that's what counts.

As usual, our two had their own way of using this slogan.

Once, on a long boring trip, they got into a typical sibling argument about nothing. I didn't pay much attention until they began trading insults and, worse still, annoying the driver, their father.

"Hey, gang," I cautioned, "remember A Soft Answer Turns Away Wrath."

"Okay, Mom!" was what they said.

What they did was happily continue the insults, in a whisper, their version of a "Soft Answer." By joining forces to deliberately misunderstand me, they removed the venom from their argument, continuing strictly out of habit.

"You know very well that's not the kind of Soft Answer I meant," I said, struggling to restrain my laughter and maintain my dignity.

They had no intention of rising to the bait by asking what I did mean. Instead they demonstrated their thorough understanding of it.

"Nancy, dear," drawled my son, "although you have questioned my manners, my rearing and my integrity, I find you overwhelmingly delightful and shall dance at your wedding—if you ever find someone who will have you."

"How kind of you to say so," murmured his sister. "I have never known a gentleman of so much wit and distinction. Have I ever told you how clever you appear to those who have no discernment?"

"No fair," he protested. "You can't use words I don't understand."

"If you two don't cut that out, I'll give you both something you will understand," growled their father.

In spite of their nonsense, they got the message that a Soft Answer not only saves trouble, it's a form of victory over your opponent. Few people can manage to maintain an argument in the face of a Soft Answer. It takes the wind out of their sails and leaves them floundering for a way to react.

I'll never forget the day a man came into our newspaper office, angrily assuring me, "I'm going to sue! This letter you printed about me is libel. It practically accuses me of bribery."

For very good reasons I despised this man. I wanted to say, "Fine, so sue me, but get out of my office because you're the most despicable person I've ever known."

Instead, I found myself answering gently, "I know how you feel. I don't like it when people write critical things about me, either. I've often wanted to sue, but it's not easy to get a libel ruling against a newspaper. Suing me will just waste your money." (Not to mention mine, I thought.)

He stood and glared at me for a few minutes, then turned to leave. "I'm still going to sue," he said, but there was little conviction in his voice and we heard no more about it.

My dear husband is good at Soft Answers. In our early years of marriage, I often became indignant over some small slight. He would hear me out as I ranted and raved and then, when I wound down, give me a look of loving patience and say, "Do you really mean that?" Of course I didn't, not really.

No wonder our grown son has been able to report several discussions with his bosses ending with his Soft Answer Turning Away Wrath—a very good idea when you are talking to the person who signs your pay check.

A Soft Answer Turns Away Wrath is so obvious, you have to wonder why everybody doesn't know it and do it. And yet, we found it one of the hardest things to teach our children—or to remember ourselves.

Gossip is mean, nasty, hateful, destructive ....
and starts at an early age.

Name calling is just as bad.

Even the youngest can understand; even the
oldest need to be reminded:

"IF YOU CAN'T SAY SOMETHING NICE— DON'T SAY ANYTHING!"

Habitual gossips are the loneliest people in the
world, but kind words collect friends.

Saint Paul said, *"Whatever is true, whatever
is noble, whatever is right, whatever is pure,
whatever is lovely, whatever is admirable —
if anything is excellent or praiseworthy —
think about such things."*

Philippians 4:8 NIV

"If You Can't Say Something Nice— Don't Say Anything"

He called himself the "Peanut Man" when he came to talk to us at Alexander Four School in Macon, Georgia. That's all I remember, except he was funny and kept us laughing. There's one thing more. Always, right in the middle of things, he would suddenly say, "If you can't say something nice…" Here he would pause dramatically, screw up his face and wait for absolute quiet from the squirming children. Then, when he had our complete attention, he'd add, "…don't say anything!"

I guess he was what would now be called a motivational speaker. At the time, I thought he was just a nice man who enjoyed children and wanted to entertain us and make us laugh. That's a possibility. At any rate, I never forgot his trade mark "saying." The other children remembered it, too. On his second visit, when he said, "If you can't say something nice…" a room full of children shouted, "…don't say anything!"

No wonder I remembered it all those years later when our two little ones learned to be critical.

Have you noticed how early this happens? Almost as soon as we learn to talk, we become critics. "Grannie, why does that lady sing so funny?" was one of our grandson Heath's first questions. "My brother is a messy eater." "The Sunday School teacher smells bad."

They're merciless!

Everyone knows what this world needs is fewer critics and more…what? Complimentors, affirmers, people who say nice things? It's a sad commentary that the English language really has no satisfactory term for the opposite of critic. The opposite of criticism is praise, but whoever heard of a "praiser?"

Our "Peanut Man" did not let this deficit in the English language deter him. We didn't either. We gave the children opportunities to express dismay and frustration with the people in their lives, but we still tried to opt for praise in preference to criticism. "If You Can't Say Something Nice, Don't Say Anything," came in handy when they began needlessly carping, especially about each other.

It's an uphill battle. For some reason, criticism comes more easily than praise. But praise is worth the effort because it makes life so much more pleasant for the recipient. It also makes the "praiser" a very congenial person to be around, especially if the praise is sincere and deserved.

The most creative "praiser" I have ever known is my friend, Martha. She not only takes the time to compliment her friends, she does it in a unique way. A lover of poetry, she picks a poem that reminds her of a friend, memorizes it and, at an appropriate time, recites it as a gift. The poem she "gave" me stands out as one of the most memorable gifts of my life.

> It's about a small bird and it concludes with,
> "...as a bird on a storm tossed branch,
> still sings,
> knowing it has wings."

When my life gets stormy, I remember Martha and the poem, and praise God for the wings of my faith in Him which keep me unafraid in the storm.

We tried to teach Nancy and Berle the gentle art of paying creative compliments. At the very least we insisted, "If You Can't Say Something Nice, Don't Say Anything!"

All children should be taught good manners and polite language for their own sake.

Maybe they don't need to spend much time with children who are rude and crude.

Nevertheless, it's easy to waste time and energy getting upset over the behavior of others. It's much better to say:

"DON'T LOOK AT ME — I DIDN'T RAISE HIM/HER"

People who let other people's behavior spoil their day can spoil the day for everyone else.

Ask them, "If you didn't raise him, why worry about it?"

"It's not my baby, I'm not gonna rock it."
Old South saying

"Don't Look At Me—I Didn't Raise Him"

One of Mother's favorite stories was about the governor's wife who was presiding at an elegant, formal dinner. Seated to her right was the guest of honor, a brilliant statesman and politician whose crude language was only exceeded by his atrocious manners. He splattered his soup, cursed liberally, and wiped his fingers on the tablecloth, leaving his napkin untouched. During the meal, nearby diners looked on with shock and distaste. As the governor's wife left the table, one of the dinner guests waylaid her. "Wasn't that awful," she said. "I've never seen such dreadful manners. Weren't you just embarrassed to death?"

"Certainly not," said the governor's wife. "Why should I care about his table manners? I Didn't Raise Him."

Mother, who didn't hesitate to lecture perfect strangers on the rudeness of their ways, took a perverse liking to this phrase. She was fond of saying, "Don't Blame Me—I Didn't Raise Him," even when commenting on the behavior of her own children.

She also used this in reverse. One Christmas vacation, Roger, our handsome neighbor, offered to drive me home from church. As we arrived at the door, Mother called, "Please go get your brother. He's working at the post office and has just thirty minutes for lunch."

Not knowing a branch post office had recently opened nearby, we drove three miles to town, looked in vain for Brother at the main post office, and came home to find him enjoying lunch at Mother's table. I was embarrassed. "What am I going to tell Roger?" I asked.

"Don't tell him anything," Mother answered with a jaunty air. "He's Not To Blame—He Didn't Raise Us."

In spite of Mother's confusing use of the phrase, we found it helpful with our kids. "Terry is disgusting," said Berle. "He wears that old, dirty hat even in the classroom."

"Don't worry about it, Honey," I said, "You Didn't Raise Him."

"Becky uses such foul language, I can't stand being on a committee with her," Nancy complained.

"It's not your problem," I told her. "You Didn't Raise Her."

People who are forever criticizing other people's behavior can be crashing bores. They can also become enormously self-righteous. To avoid this, it helps to remember, "I Didn't Raise Him."

"Don't Look At Me—I Didn't Raise Him" is a great conversation stopper. On one rare occasion my mother-in-law was complaining about Himself, her practically perfect son. Without thinking, I said, "Don't Look At Me—I Didn't Raise Him."

Her complaints came to a sputtering stop. Finally she managed, "Well, I thought I had done a better job."

She got even with me on our twenty-fifth wedding anniversary. In the midst of all the congratulations on our "long and happy" marriage, she leaned over, patted her fifty-year-old son on the shoulder and said to me, "Now! You've had him as long as I did. If there's anything wrong with him from now on, it's your fault."

Not on your life. I didn't raise him!

Half the problems in the world....more than half... are caused by simple misunderstandings.

If we only knew what the other person is *thinking, feeling, wanting...*

...If they only knew what we were *thinking, feeling, wanting....*

...How much kinder and gentler and more helpful we would be to one another.

If we could only learn, and teach our children to:

"GIVE THEM THE BENEFIT OF THE DOUBT"

When a teacher yells, or a friend sulks, or a hero fails them, remind them, gently, "Give them the benefit of the doubt."

Or as Jesus commands: *"Do not judge or you too will be judged."*

Matthew 7:1 NIV

"Give Them The Benefit Of The Doubt"

Berle stomped into the kitchen, banging the door behind him. "My teacher is trying to choose my friends for me." He slammed his books on the kitchen table. You could almost see the steam coming out his ears. "She forced me to move my seat away from my friend. That's not fair!"

"She must have had a reason," I suggested, as mildly as I could.

"Sure she did," he said. "She hates me." (This of a teacher who had known and loved him since he was knee-high to a grasshopper.)

"Come on now," I said. "Give Her The Benefit Of The Doubt. How many times has she told you and Peter not to talk to each other while she's teaching?"

"Only once," he said, then added sheepishly, "Today."

"What about last week?"

"Well, maybe once or twice."

"Is it barely possible she asked you to move so both of you would learn to pay attention?" I asked. "Why don't you assume that's what it is until you have further evidence that she hates you?"

"I'll try," he muttered, "but I still say she wants to choose my friends."

"Lucky you!" I couldn't help it. His teacher, a dear friend of mine, loved Berle like a son.

Later—much later—he confessed that his friend, Peter, had been a disruptive influence. "She did me a favor when she moved me," he said. "He could have gotten me into serious trouble."

Anger is bad for you, without a doubt. It raises the blood pressure, distracts the mind and destroys relationships. If you give it a natural outlet in vengeance, it leads to guilt or punishment, or both. If you try to ignore it, it turns inwards and, over time, damages your health and mental well-being. How much better to convert it into understanding, sympathy, or even pity—emotions that do no harm to the nervous system and can restore relationships.

Easy to say! Hard to do, much less teach your children. Our way was to remind them to Give Them The Benefit Of The Doubt. Whenever the children were hurt, or grieved, or angered by someone's actions or words, we tried to remember to suggest they look for a reason behind it.

"Maybe Mrs. Jones had a headache today or she wouldn't have yelled at you."

"Do you think Barbara really intended to snub you, or was she just in a hurry to get to class?"

As with many of our slogans, the children sometimes used this one to communicate with us in difficult circumstances. During Nancy's Junior High years, she and her good friend, Jane, both liked a handsome young man named David. One day, Nancy talked at length on the phone with Jane. A few minutes later the phone rang and Nancy answered it. She handed it to me, saying with a look of concern, "It's for you, Mother. Please Give Me The Benefit Of The Doubt." (Do you know how many horrors can enter your mind between putting your hand on the phone and getting it to your ear? Plenty!)

The call was from Jane's mother. She told me Jane's brother reported he had spied the girls passing a note to David on the school bus. I knew about the note. It was an invitation from the girls to a picnic they had planned.

Jane was reprimanded for passing notes, but Nancy had asked for The Benefit Of The Doubt. This helped me stop a moment and remember what it was like to be Junior High age, with the first shy budding of social involvement. I saw no particular harm in passing notes on a school bus. In fact, I suddenly recalled passing a few myself.

(I did take the opportunity to point out to Nancy that it was easier to Give Her The Benefit Of The Doubt because she had communicated with me about the picnic. I tried never to miss a chance to let our kids know it was important to communicate.)

My mother had another version of giving people the benefit of the doubt:

"Honey," she told me, when I complained of a friend who hurt my feelings, "the people who set out to hurt your feelings on purpose are few. Most of the time they're so occupied with wondering what you think of them, they don't have time to think up ways to hurt you."

Whether or not this is true, I've found believing it is most convenient. If I Give Them The Benefit Of The Doubt, then I don't waste time and energy wondering what I did to deserve their meanness. I don't have to bother with ways to get even. It also deprives them of the satisfaction of making me unhappy, if indeed that had been their aim.

In the long run, I have found that giving people the benefit of the doubt, whether they deserve it or not, makes life more pleasant for me. If it also makes it pleasant for them—fine!

You don't want to scare them to death, but sometimes it takes that final threat to get their attention.

They have to believe that if they don't behave, **something dreadful** is going to happen.

Because, if they don't learn to behave when they're kids, **something dreadful** *will* happen when they're older.

There are lots of ways to do it. Teachers use "the principal's office."

We tried: "If you don't behave yourself there will be

"SCRUDGINS"

You don't know what "scrudgins" is?

Lucky you! Pray you never find out!

"You don't have to be crazy to belong to this family, but it sure helps."

Family motto

"Scrudgins"

Helena, my Canadian friend who successfully raised six children, had to get up early in the morning to stay ahead of her lively brood. They were not only physically energetic, their mental wheels were always whirring. So were hers!

"No problem," Helena says, when you ask about disciplining this bunch. "I just tell them, 'Stop that or there will be SCRUDGINS.' Then I add, 'Oh, you don't know what SCRUDGINS is? Lucky you!' That slows them down a bit," she concludes cheerfully. "Long enough for me to take cover."

My two paid no more attention to a threat of SCRUDGINS than, I suspect, did Helena's. In fact, the time I tried it, out of the corner of my eye I spied them giving each other the universal signal for "Mother's lost her marbles!"

Every family needs a "line drawn in the sand" signal that Mother— or Father—is getting close to the final straw. For some mothers it's, "Your father will hear about this." But that works only if the father really is an ogre. It has to be something that's the equivalent of the teacher's time honored threat of the trip to the principal's office, although that, too, can lose its sting. The only time Berle went to the principal's office, he lost all fear of it. He knew and liked the principal and didn't mind a bit sitting and watching the other youngsters come in and get their comeuppance.

Some mothers choose the countdown method: "I'm going to count to three…" It's amazing how often this, like SCRUDGINS, works. A young mother, employed at our newspaper, had two young daughters who spent the last two hours of each working day at home alone. She kept in touch by telephone. One afternoon Number Two Daughter called and complained about a work assignment she had been given. As she protested, her mother said, "Kathy, I don't want to hear any more about this. I'm going to count to three. One, two…."

She came away from the phone, laughing. "I can't believe that," she said. "I'm two miles away. What could I have done if I had counted to three?"

"Gone home and spanked her," suggested my favorite disciplinarian from behind his desk.

Children who are threatened with SCRUDGINS, or even their father, are better off than children whose parents simply give in rather than call a halt. All the experts agree kids need that control, that boundary to let them know someone in charge cares about how they behave. Look at the children around you! It's easy to tell whose parents draw the line, and whose don't. SCRUDGINS is a fun way to do it.

Worrying is a bad habit that should be broken as early as possible. It's a trait which is easily handed down from generation to generation. Don't encourage it.

Help children say, "What's the worst that could happen?" It's usually not much to worry about.

Don't let them worry in secret; get them to talk about it, then *assure them,*

"WORRY IS LIKE A ROCKING CHAIR— IT GIVES YOU SOMETHING TO DO BUT IT DOESN'T GET YOU ANYWHERE"

Jesus said, *"Who of you by worrying can add a single hour to his life?"*

Matthew 6:27 NIV

"Worry Is Like A Rocking Chair—It Gives You Something To Do But It Doesn't Get You Anywhere"

You've seen the bumper stickers and buttons. "Why Worry?" they ask. "Who, me worry?" People who worry see it as the natural state of mankind. The people who live with them try to think of ways to make them cease. Unless, of course, they help them worry. You know what I mean.

"Hey, Harry, nice day!"

"Yeah, but I bet it rains by evening. It'll ruin the crops."

"Mary, your children are charming, so well behaved and polite."

"That's because they're not teenagers yet. I know they'll be impossible by the time they get in high school."

This is a disabling habit, one that can be passed down from generation to generation. Believing this, I tried mightily to throw off the worry habit which my Grandmother unwittingly taught me. I didn't want our children to be worrywarts, so I had to conquer my habit. No danger of their learning to worry from Himself. If he ever worried, no one knew it.

I confess I wasn't making much headway until the United States Marine Corps, in its wisdom, sent my husband off to combat in Vietnam. With daily headlines and grizzly details of the awful things going on where my beloved was located, my worry habit shifted into high gear.

Very quickly I acknowledged, "That way lies madness!" After a miserable month of trying to turn off my imagination and stop worrying, I knew I couldn't do it on my own. I placed the whole thing in God's hands. That helped! Although I never completely stopped worrying, I did stop borrowing so much trouble and managed to make it through the year with my sanity intact.

After that it was easier for me to urge the children not to worry. I like, "Worry Is Like A Rocking Chair—It Gives You Something To

Do, But It Doesn't Get You Anywhere." Borrowed from my brother-in-law, this little saying not only suggests you not worry, but points out the uselessness of it.

Grandmother would not have agreed with this. She was a very creative worrier. Constantly teased by the family because of the quantity and variety of her worrying, she finally said, "Don't tell me it doesn't help to worry. Look at all the things I worried about that didn't happen."

Very few of us have perfect features or perfect figures. We waste time wishing we were more beautiful. Even beautiful people waste time trying to be more beautiful. At first, we don't want to hear

"PRETTY IS AS PRETTY DOES, MAY YOU ALWAYS BE BEAUTIFUL"

When we realize we will never reach our ideal outer beauty,

We start working on the inner beauty that doesn't fade.

A beautiful face may win friends, but beautiful behavior holds them.

Children who learn that "Pretty is as pretty does" develop a self-confidence the "ravages of time" cannot erode — plus the satisfaction of making their own beauty.

St. Peter wrote, *"Your beauty should not come from outward adornment, such as braided hair and the wearing of gold jewelry and fine clothes. Instead, it should be that of your inner self, the unfading beauty of a gentle and quiet spirit, which is of great worth in God's sight."*

1 Peter 3:3 NIV

"Pretty Is As Pretty Does— May You Always Be Beautiful"

One of the most beautiful people I have ever known is truly homely. Her face is long and large. None of her features fit with any other. Her hair is thin and wispy. No two strands seem to go in the same direction. You have the impression she no longer gives it more than a pat into place, knowing it won't stay. She has lots of friends, and people go out of their way to spend time in her company. You don't even notice her looks. In fact, I wasn't aware she was homely until I saw a picture of her. Stilled by the camera, her pale blue eyes failed to reflect the kindness they showed in person; her words of concern and humor were silenced.

This delightful human being is likely to show up at my back fence unexpectedly, somehow knowing that I have a cold. "Please try my new recipe for chicken soup," she says. "I'm not sure about a new ingredient I put in it."

She is also expert at preparing light and fluffy gelatin dishes that go down with no effort and provide plenty of nourishment. Flowers from her garden or a book she can't wait to share are also part of her generosity. She has an endless collection of small jokes, mostly told on herself, but, if you want to do the talking, she is an avid listener. She is one of my favorite people and a shining example of Pretty Is As Pretty Does.

I didn't like it when Grandmother told me, "Pretty Is As Pretty Does—May You Always Be Beautiful," possibly because she usually said it when I was acting in an unbeautiful way. I didn't want to *act* beautiful. I wanted to *be* beautiful, with blonde curls and a turned-up nose and pale, fair skin, like Shirley Temple. For years, I ignored the fact that this would never happen. Dark hair and eyes, freckles, and what my friends called a year-round tan could not be changed. I didn't want to think about it.

Words, like water, have a way of making a permanent impact, so, by the time it mattered, Grandmother's insistence that Pretty Is As

Pretty Does, along with reminders that, "You need to be more lady-like," had taken their toll. I accepted the fact that my one chance to be beautiful was in my behavior.

This saying made young Nancy as angry as it did me.

"Mother, why are you punishing me? All I did was hang up on her. She was being a real pest and I told her good-bye three times before I hung up. Besides, she started it."

"Maybe she did," I responded, "but she's not my responsibility—you are. You did more than just hang up, you slammed the phone down. No matter the provocation, you did an ugly thing and I don't want you to be ugly. I want you to be beautiful and...."

"Pretty Is As Pretty Does." We finished the sentence together. Nancy's voice was tinged with resentment. Never mind, she got the message.

- If they yell back when people yell at them—
- If they become a grouch when in the company of grouches—
- If their smile can be erased by another's frown—

...they need to learn not to allow themselves to be affected or controlled by others.

It's hard to explain and it's still harder to do.

Try, "If someone is unpleasant, unfriendly or thoughtless, show them how it's done: be pleasant, be friendly, be thoughtful."

"DON'T BE HIS ROBOT"

"Don't let him punch your buttons. Don't let him make you unpleasant, unfriendly, thoughtless. You set the mood!"

"Don't give another permission to determine your behavior."
Uncle Cliff

"Don't Be His Robot"

"She makes me so mad!" Nancy, not her usual calm and collected self, banged down the phone.

"Who makes you so mad?"

"That fink, Sarah!"

"Fink?" I asked, in my most reproving voice. "What kind of name is that to call someone?"

"It's not bad enough for Sarah!"

Nancy, my Nancy, actually kicked the footstool across the room.

"Honey, don't do that." Without thinking, I picked up the stool, noting with mild satisfaction that Nancy was paying for her burst of temper with a hurt toe.

"Mother, she calls me names and tells tales on everybody at school. Jane says she called me a stuck-up floozy and said I had a bad temper."

"That wasn't very nice, but why are you Being Her Robot?"

"Being Her Robot?"

"That's what I said."

"What's that supposed to mean?" She wasn't sure she wanted to know.

"You're letting her push your buttons. That's what happens to robots."

"Wanna explain, Mom?"

"I thought you'd never ask." I pulled her down on the sofa beside me, gently rubbing her back.

"If Jane hadn't called and told you about Sarah, what would you be doing right now?"

"Well, I was on my way to the kitchen to get a soda. Then I planned to cut out my new dress."

"Instead, here you are, stomping all around the room, kicking innocent stools..."

"Sorry about that!" She looked sheepish.

"...and, instead of spending a quiet, pleasant afternoon, you're seething with frustration, anger, dreams of revenge, right?"

"Well, I'm not sure about the revenge, but, yes, I guess so. She makes me so mad!" Jumping up, hands on hips, she glared at me.

"Why do you let her?"

"Let her what?"

"Make you mad. If you let Sarah's actions make you mad, then she's pushing your buttons. She's controlling how you feel and act. You're Being Her Robot."

"But I can't just ignore what she said."

"Why not? Then you can go on with your sewing. You'll be controlling your own thoughts and feelings"

"But what about Sarah?"

"What about Sarah? Being a ... fink, I believe you said, is her problem, not yours. You can choose to figure out why she behaves that way, and try to help her solve her problem, or you can ignore it. Just don't let it affect how you feel and how you behave."

"What if people believe all those things she says about me?"

"Then they're her robots and it's their problem. It's still not yours. Where are you going?"

"I need milk instead of soda. This requires brain power. Maybe I'll get it figured out before I'm too old to care."

"I hope so!"

It makes sense when you think about it. I was a grown woman with a long history of being a robot to other people when I read a short story about a waitress who was always grouchy with her breakfast customers. She scowled at them and most of them scowled back. One customer unfailingly greeted her growled, "What do you want?" with, "Good morning, lovely day, isn't it?"

A friend asked why he was so pleasant to the old grouch.

"Because," he said, "I like being pleasant. Why should I let her decide that I should be grouchy?"

Wanting my children to develop this rare ability to "push their own buttons" and be in charge of themselves, regardless of the attitudes of those around them, I searched a long time for a slogan to sum this up. A movie about a robot gave me what I needed.

It's only human nature for our behavior to reflect the attitudes of people around us: to yell at people who yell at us; to snarl back when snarled at; to be friendly only with those who are friendly to us. Being your own person, regardless of how you're treated, is seldom easy. But, oh how I admire those rare people who will Be Nobody's Robot.

Typically, the kids had their own short version of this. One evening I heard Berle whisper to Nancy, "Dad's grouchy tonight. Don't let him Robot You."

During supper, Nancy was her most charming self, shamelessly buttering up her father. Very soon we had an equally charming Daddy on our hands. She had "roboted" him. I guess, come to think of it, it does work both ways.

Money can't give you a hug when you're feeling low.

Jewelry can't share a laugh when you're feeling good.

Bicycles are more fun when someone rides with you.

A big house is empty without a human voice in it.

No matter how you figure it,

"PEOPLE ARE MORE IMPORTANT THAN THINGS"

Children who learn this will never be truly poor.

People who do not know this will never be truly rich.

James Russell Lowell wrote, *"Not what we give, but what we share, for the gift without the giver is bare."*
The Vision of Sir Launfal

"People Are More Important Than Things"

People Are More Important Than Things! This one is easier "caught" than taught. It also needs to be put into words. When a treasured possession is destroyed, especially through misuse, it's hard to remember that the person who destroyed it is more important than the "thing," no matter how valuable. No wonder we hear stories of relatives or friends who let an argument over mere possessions damage their relationship.

Great Aunt Sallie Lu rather prided herself on the fact that she and her sister had not spoken for seventeen years. It began when her sister took possession of their dying mother's ring. Aunt Sallie Lu always thought it should be hers.

How can anyone let a ring cost her a sister? Sisters can comfort and advise you, laugh with you and stick up for you when the world is going wrong. Rings don't do anything but sit on your finger and look pretty—sometimes.

My good friend, Libby, offered to help clean up the kitchen after a dinner party. As we chattered away, washing dishes together, she opened a cabinet to put away a glass. Slipping from her hands, it hit the counter, wiping out two of my fine china cups and one saucer. Libby was distraught, almost to the point of tears. With one big gulp for the lost china which had been my mother's and was not replaceable, I managed to put my arms around her, saying, "Libby, you are more important to me than a whole set of china. Please don't let it upset you."

Sure enough, the china, or what's left of it, seldom leaves the shelf. It doesn't fit well with casual Florida entertaining. But Libby and I still exchange notes and visits and I cherish her friendship beyond value.

It's a challenge to help children find a happy medium between allowing friends to destroy their belongings, and teaching them that People Are More Important Than Things. Certainly a habitually destructive friend needs to be dealt with, but mistakes will happen; carelessness can be expected.

Jake was only being playful when he pretended to steal Berle's bike and headed off down the street, with Berle in loud and furious pursuit. I don't believe he meant to hit the tree. If he did, the bump on his head was adequate evidence of the error of his ways. He sat on the ground beside the crumpled bike, head in his hands, tears in his eyes, repeating, "I'm sorry! I'm sorry!"

Gazing at his battered bike, Berle found it hard to accept Jake's protestation that he didn't mean to do it.

"I know how you feel, Honey," I told him. "But the bike can be fixed and, right now, Jake is hurting more than the bike is. Try and understand that People Are More Important Than Things and go give your friend a hand up."

He did it grudgingly at first, but the two were soon laughing about how silly Jake looked running into the tree. When Jake, prompted no doubt by very wise parents, offered to pay for repairs to the bike, all was completely right again between the two pals.

We made suggestions when trouble developed with friends. We were more emphatic when it involved siblings! In the early years, I told them, "If you fight over it, it's mine!" Later I asked, "Which do you care more about, the book, or your brother?"

Sometimes Nancy would respond, "The book! Who cares about a horrid old brother!"

"You, I hope. Surely you know People Are More Important Than Things. And yes, brothers are people." I said it before she could raise the question.

Berle could be equally uncharitable. "I can get another sister," he said, "but I can't afford another shirt like that."

Undaunted, we continued to insist that they be aware that People Are More Important Than Things, hoping they'd finally get the message.

One of the most satisfying moments of my life came during a trip to Canada. Berle was given the choice of going to a Hands On Museum for children, in Toronto, or spending an extra day with his friend, Harvey, at a lakeside cottage. The museum sounded exciting, but I was gratified that Berle preferred spending time with his friend. It showed he was already learning the value of friendships.

After our parents died, my siblings and I sat down to divide up our family treasures. We all had favorite items, enhanced by special memories. Inevitably, we cherished some of the same things. How grateful I am that a lifetime of believing People Are More Important

Than Things helped us remember the most important thing inherited from our parents was a close and loving relationship with each other. My brother and sister took home a couple of pieces I wanted. I'm sure some of the family heirlooms now in my home were special to them. I don't know. They would never tell me. How grateful I am that we are more important to each other than even a whole house full of things!

"AN OUNCE OF PREVENTION............."

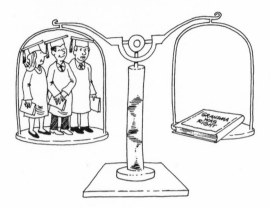

- Saves time...
- Saves money...
- Saves heartache...
- Saves frustration...
- Saves starting over...
- Saves a lot of mistakes...
- Saves friendships...
- Saves confidence...
- Saves worry...
- Saves trouble...
- Saves parental sanity... etc.

If you picture the kind of person you want them to be, you can't start too early to get them there.

If making sacrifices is necessary to "get them there," it's worth it!

"Train a child in the way he should go and when he is old he will not turn from it."

Proverbs 22:6 NIV

"An Ounce Of Prevention..."

This is only half a slogan because I know of no words to adequately explain the value of An Ounce Of Prevention when it comes to raising children. Each of us must complete the slogan for ourselves. An Ounce Of Prevention can be expensive. It can necessitate reading, from the beginning, everything you can find on raising kids, instead of waiting until something begins to go wrong. It can interfere with recreation, exercise and partying. It can even cause losing track of what's happening on the "Soaps." Applying An Ounce Of Prevention can also interfere with a budding career in business for either mother or father.

Of course, it's never too late to start, but starting early to teach children the attitudes that will get them triumphantly through life makes your task easier in the long run.

When Nancy was barely three, we lived beside an enclosed courtyard, shared with eleven other couples, mostly young families like us. The children roamed freely around the courtyard and all the mothers kept an eye out for all the kids. Nancy knew she was not to go inside anyone's house without permission and I seldom worried about her. She was always in sight from my kitchen window.

Then Mother came to visit. After the greetings were over, I looked around for Nancy. She was nowhere to be found. I checked in all the houses on the court with no success, while Mother watched anxiously from my doorway. Calling Nancy's name, I turned the corner into unfamiliar territory and a small voice said, "Here me is, Mommy."

There she was, popping out of a house she'd never been in before, proud as punch to be answering my call. Leading her back across the courtyard, I chided her for disobedience, gently, so she wouldn't greet her grandmother with a torrent of tears. Moments later, when Grandmother needed to go shopping, I told Nancy she couldn't go, making clear it was punishment for going in a house without permission. We left her wailing on the doorstep, her father playing reluctant jailor.

I felt terrible.

"I'm sorry, Mother. I hate to start your visit by disciplining your grandchild and leaving her in tears."

She gave me one of her wonderful smiles. "I can handle the tears," she said. "I'm delighted to find you've learned one of the most important points of parenting."

"Really? What's that?"

"Time spent now teaching Nancy you mean what you say—that she has to obey you—is time saved later when it's even more important. Every time she gets away with ignoring you it takes that much longer to show her you mean it."

A few weeks later, a neighbor underscored this for me. "Your Nancy is a character," she said. "She was in my house the other day, and you called her from your doorway. She didn't even look up, so I told her you were calling.

"'I know,' she said. Then you called again and I asked, 'Aren't you going to answer her?' You'll never believe what she said."

"Tell me."

"She said, 'It's all right. If she really wants me, she'll come get me.' Can you believe that?"

"Yes," I said, picturing a dozen situations in which Nancy could get into serious trouble by not answering my call, and waiting for me to come get her. "But that's going to change," I promised myself.

"An Ounce of Prevention..." may be only half a slogan, but how parents complete it will make all the difference in the world to the future well-being of their children.

"I love you." Everyone needs to hear these words.

"I love you." No other words will do.

Without them, loving relationships are never complete.

Without them, life is barren and pointless.

"I love you." Deeds of love are not enough without the words.

"I love you." Words of love are not enough without the deeds.

If you never say another thing to your children, don't fail to say

"I LOVE YOU"

St. Paul says, *"If I give all I possess to the poor and surrender my body to the flames, but have not love, I gain nothing."*
1 Corinthians 13:3 NIV

"I Love You"

"I Love You!" Yes, I know it's not a slogan, but no home should be without it. Stories are plentiful of grown-ups who have never heard these words from a parent. The mother—or father—may have shown them love in all other ways, but it isn't enough. They yearn to hear the words, "I love you!"

Why are these words so hard to say? Why are they so important?

Tell them, "I Love You," and they'll obey not only your commands, but your wishes.

When I told my daddy that a young man had asked me to elope with him, he turned his big blue eyes on me and said, "Honey, I Love You. You wouldn't do that to your old daddy, would you?"

I didn't reply. If I had, it would have been, "Never, not if it would hurt you."

Tell them, "I Love You," and their sense of belonging will help keep them safe from doing drugs, smoking, drinking, promiscuous sex, or any other acts that tempt insecure people.

"Come on, Anne," said my date, "one little drink won't hurt you. Everybody else is drinking." Nearby friends took up the invitation, "Come on, have a drink!"

I'll never know what I might have done. A commanding voice quickly silenced the crowd. My sister, her own glass of wine beside her plate, said, "Leave her alone! If she doesn't want a drink, she doesn't want a drink. Stop pestering her."

I didn't need to belong to their crowd. I had my own!

Tell them, "I Love You," and their feelings of self worth will carry them through.

Nancy was fourth runner-up in the school's beauty pageant. "Do you mind not being the beauty queen of Lejeune High?" I asked.

"I don't think so," she replied, smiling over her nosegays, one from us—one from Ben, who, I suspect, had already told her he loved her.

"I know whose beauty queen I am," she said.

Tevye, the lead character in the movie *Fiddler On The Roof*, watches in amazement as his daughters marry for love, refusing the mates chosen by matchmaker and parents. Finally he begins to wonder. In one of the best scenes of the movie, he asks Golde, his wife of many years, "Do you love me?"

She can't believe he's asking. Their marriage was arranged and they were strangers when they wed. They've been together for thirty years, for pity's sake. She rattles off a list of things they've done together, including having three daughters, plus all the things she does for him. When she pauses for breath, he says, "Yes, but do you love me?" Thirty years and they never said the words.

Tell them, "I Love You," and you give them wings with which to fly and roots to bring them home again.

Even parents who never heard "I Love You" from their parents— *especially* parents who never heard "I Love You" from their parents— need to push past the barrier, hold out their arms, hug that kid and say, "I Love You!"

It's like the boys used to say about kissing a girl. "After the first, the rest comes easy."

Index of Challenges

ORDER FORM

Please send me:

____ Copies of *Grandma Was Right!* @ $11.95 per copy _____

    California residents add 8.25% tax   _____

    Postage and handling for one copy $2.00

    Postage and handling for additional
copies @ 75¢ each   _____

    TOTAL ENCLOSED   _____

SHIP TO:

NAME _____

ADDRESS _____

CITY _____ STATE _____ ZIP _____

Please make checks payable to:

Studio 4 Productions

P.O. Box 280400
Northridge, CA 91328-0400